HIP-HOP TURNTABLISM, CREATIVITY AND COLLABORATION

UNIVERSITY OF
WINCHESTER

Martial Rose Library
Tel: **01962 827306**

To be returned on or before the day marked above, subject to recall.

Hip-Hop Turntablism, Creativity and Collaboration

SOPHY SMITH
De Montfort University, Leicester, UK

Routledge
Taylor & Francis Group

LONDON AND NEW YORK

First published 2013 by Ashgate Publishing

2 Park Square, Milton Park, Abingdon, Oxon OX14 4RN
711 Third Avenue, New York, NY 10017, USA

Routledge is an imprint of the Taylor & Francis Group, an informa business

First issued in paperback 2016

British Library Cataloguing in Publication Data
Smith, Sophy.
  Hip-hop turntablism, creativity and collaboration. --
  (Ashgate popular and folk music series)
  1. Turntablism. 2. Turntablists. 3. Rap (Music)--History
  and criticism.
  I. Title II. Series
  781.6'49132-dc23

The Library of Congress has cataloged the printed edition as follows:
Smith, Sophy.
  Hip-hop turntablism, creativity and collaboration / by Sophy Smith.
      p. cm. -- (Ashgate popular and folk music series)
  Includes bibliographical references and index.
  ISBN 978-1-4094-4337-7 (hardback)
Turntablism. 2. Hip-hop. I. Title.
  ML3531.S65 2013
  782.421649--dc23

                                                                    2012030315

ISBN 978-1-4094-4337-7 (hbk)
ISBN 978-1-138-25461-9 (pbk)

Contents

List of Figures   vii
List of Tables   ix
General Editor's Preface   xi
Acknowledgements   xiii

1   Introduction   1

2   Hip-Hop and Collaboration   9

3   Turntablism in Context   15

4   Turntablism and Technology   29

5   The Creation of Original Sound Material   43

6   Team Formation and the Creative Processes
     of Hip-Hop Turntable Teams   51

7   An Analytical Methodology for Hip-Hop Turntable Music   71

8   Notation and Transcription Techniques   81

9   Analysis of the Compositional Process of UK Hip-Hop Teams   103

10   Conclusion   147

Bibliography   151
Index   163

List of Figures

8.1   Webber's notation for the movement of the record
      and the direction of the hand on the turntable   86
8.2   Webber's notation for fader movement   86
8.3   Webber's notation for articulation   87
8.4   Webber's staff   87
8.5   Carluccio, Imboden and Pirtle's notation for the rotation
      and distance of travel of the record   88
8.6   Carluccio, Imboden and Pirtle's notation for the movement
      of the record   89
8.7   The five main functions of hip-hop turntable notation   93
8.8   A score for the notation of hip-hop turntable routines 96
8.9   The staff, subdivided into bars and beats   97
8.10 The rotation of the record versus time   98

List of Tables

6.1   Model framework of the devising process   70

7.1   Tagg's 'Checklist of parameters of musical expression'   74
7.2   Hawkins' 'Basic types of compositional features'   75
7.3   Moore's 'Stratified layer model'   75
7.4   Wall's 'Elements for analysing popular music meanings'   76
7.5   Framework for the analysis of hip-hop team turntable composition   78

8.1   Doc Rice's three categories of fader movement   85
8.2   Doc Rice's notation for the directional movement of the record   85
8.3   The depiction of sound manipulation techniques   99
8.4   Depiction of sample material   99
8.5   The depiction of other occurrences   100

9.1   Duration of individual sections within the routine   112
9.2   Time signature and tempo of individual sections   112
9.3   Sample types used in the routine   113
9.4   DMU Crew: Manipulation techniques and their users   116
9.5   Duration of individual sections within the routine   123
9.6   Time signature and tempo of sections   123
9.7   Sample types used in the routine   124
9.8   Length of sections within the three-section structure   125
9.9   Length of sections within the four-section structure   125
9.10   The Mixologists: Manipulation techniques and their users   127
9.11   Duration of individual sections within the routine   132
9.12   Time signature and tempo of sections   132
9.13   Sample types used in the routine   133
9.14   The Scratch Perverts: Manipulation techniques and their users   136

General Editor's Preface

The upheaval that occurred in musicology during the last two decades of the twentieth century has created a new urgency for the study of popular music alongside the development of new critical and theoretical models. A relativistic outlook has replaced the universal perspective of modernism (the international ambitions of the 12-note style); the grand narrative of the evolution and dissolution of tonality has been challenged, and emphasis has shifted to cultural context, reception and subject position. Together, these have conspired to eat away at the status of canonical composers and categories of high and low in music. A need has arisen, also, to recognize and address the emergence of crossovers, mixed and new genres, to engage in debates concerning the vexed problem of what constitutes authenticity in music and to offer a critique of musical practice as the product of free, individual expression.

Popular musicology is now a vital and exciting area of scholarship, and the *Ashgate Popular and Folk Music Series* presents some of the best research in the field. Authors are concerned with locating musical practices, values and meanings in cultural context, and draw upon methodologies and theories developed in cultural studies, semiotics, poststructuralism, psychology and sociology. The series focuses on popular musics of the twentieth and twenty-first centuries. It is designed to embrace the world's popular musics from Acid Jazz to Zydeco, whether high tech or low tech, commercial or non-commercial, contemporary or traditional.

Professor Derek B. Scott
Professor of Critical Musicology
University of Leeds

Acknowledgements

I could not have conducted this research nor written this book without the generous help and support of so many people. Shout outs to LLTJ, Yoshi C and Stevie P for their huge support and, very importantly, my mum and dad. Massive thanks go to all the turntable team members who shared their music with me, especially members of The Mixologists, the Scratch Perverts and the DMU Crew as well as all the internet forum members who shared their thoughts and love of hip-hop.

I am grateful to the following for permission to reproduce original work in this book: Kimi 'Doc Rice' Ushida (tables 8.1 and 8.2); Berklee Press (figures 8.1, 8.2, 8.3 and 8.4 [from *Turntable Technique* (2000) © Stephen Webber and Berklee Press]); and John Carluccio (figures 8.5 and 8.6 [from John Carluccio/ TTM: Turntable Transcription Methodology © (2000), www.ttmethod.com]).

Chapter 1

Introduction

This book studies the compositional processes of turntable teams working within the hip-hop genre to collectively compose original music using turntables. Since the development of the gramophone at the end of the nineteenth century, the turntable has become an instrument of creation as well as reproduction, changing the shape of music history (Poschardt, 1998, p. 235). This has led to the groundbreaking compositional strategies of hip-hop turntablism, including the development of creative sound manipulation techniques and flexible compositional processes. Poschardt regards the progressive compositional processes inherent in hip-hop turntable music as making the genre one of the final avant-gardes of the twentieth century (p. 392). For me, this is an important area to study as little work has been undertaken so far into the innovative work of groups of DJs working in popular culture. Although the turntable work of art music composers such as John Cage and Pierre Schaeffer is relatively well known among the academic music community, little scholarly work has been undertaken into the equally interesting turntable music taking place in popular culture. The key contribution of this book is in the development of an analytical methodology specifically for turntable music. The development of a model framework for analysing compositional process, as well as a new notation expressly for the analysis of turntable music, allows an exploration of the creative processes of hip-hop turntable teams by analysing both the process and the artistic product that results from that process. In doing so, this book establishes characteristics of compositional process and style and looks at the features that unite the routines without flattening their distinctions.

Previous work on hip-hop music has fallen into two camps – either sociological studies that focus on the representation of race or the creation of identity in popular culture (Rose, 1994 and Dimitriadis, 2001) or cultural and historical studies that chart the development of hip-hop music through interviews with influential DJs (Brewster and Broughton, 1999 and Poschardt, 1998). The sociological studies take an academic approach whereas the cultural and historical studies tend to be more journalistic. Brewster and Broughton are extremely derisive of any academic scholarship into DJ culture (p. 20), but Poschardt does explore some cultural and theoretical contexts. There have been a number of short works written concerning DJing in live performance (White, 1996 and Allen, 1997) and one book concerning sample-based hip-hop created in a studio context (Schloss, 2004), but by and large the actual music of live hip-hop has been neglected. Schloss comments on how the aesthetic goals of hip-hop artists have been excluded from academic work (p. 2), asserting that most hip-hop scholars have emerged from disciplines concerned with the study of text or social processes rather than musical structures and are not interested in the actual music. This book aims to fill these 'blank spaces' (Schloss, p. 2) and to demonstrate that hip-hop music is worth academic attention not just in its role within popular culture, but as music itself. This book offers a new approach to hip-hop scholarship not only because it focuses on the music itself, but because in order to do so it presents an analytical methodology and notation system that are suitable for the analysis of hip-hop turntable composition.

The Turntable Teams

Three turntable teams are studied in detail in this book, all of which were based in the UK – The DMU Crew (based in Leicester), the Mixologists (based in London) and the Scratch Perverts (based in London). These three teams were chosen for specific reasons. The Mixologists and the Scratch Perverts are both internationally renowned professional turntable teams who have been established for a number of years. The routines chosen for analysis are examples of hip-hop turntable music at the highest level. Although the third team, the DMU Crew, included a number of professional DJs, the team itself does not work professionally and the routine studied was completed early in the team's formation. The contrast in the abilities of these three groups enabled me to gain a wider picture of the processes of hip-hop turntable teams than would have been possible if only the established, professional teams were analysed. This approach will demonstrate how compositional processes are similar across the UK hip-hop turntablist community, regardless of the level of the team in either ability or status.

Because all three teams are based in the UK they could be accessed easily for both interviews and performances. It was vital to my research to have as much contact and discussion with the teams as possible. Schloss feels that the aesthetics of hip-hop composition can only be studied fully from within the hip-hop community and sees this as lacking in much research, commenting, 'Most researchers who have written about hip-hop have not sought or have not gained access to that community' (p. 21). To fulfil my aim of writing about the composition of hip-hop team turntable music, as well as the resulting artistic product, it was necessary for me to get as close to the creative processes of the teams as possible which meant accessing and participating in the community. Because the DMU Crew had just formed they were happy to grant me full access to their compositional process, which was invaluable for the success of this research. The Mixologists were also extremely open and gave extensive interviews about their process and would have given direct access to their rehearsals and process had their scheduling allowed it. The Scratch Perverts, the most well known of the teams, were positive about the research into their work but were unable to give direct access to their process due to their professional commitments. Because of this, the majority of research about them is interview-based.

The gender split of the teams was extremely one-sided. Only one of the team members is female, reflecting the gender bias in this area of hip-hop as a whole. The ethnicity of team members is also extremely biased. The majority of team members are white; one is Asian. In my approach to ethnicity in this study, I share the view of Schloss who does not specify ethnicity when discussing hip-hop musicians and their creative work in *Making Beats* (2004). Making such distinctions, he feels, would be distorting, as the difference in ethnic background does not manifest itself in any stylistic difference between the practices of hip-hop musicians:

> All producers – regardless of race – make African American hip-hop. And those who do it well are respected, largely without regard to their ethnicity. (pp. 9–10)

Hip-hop, he says, is African American music regardless of the ethnicity of its creators:

> ... African-derived aesthetics, social norms, standards and sensibilities are deeply embedded in the form, even when it is being performed by individuals who are not themselves of African descent. (p. 3)

The Background to Hip-Hop Turntablism and Some Definitions

In the early 1970s, a 'new and revolutionary genre' (Brewster and Broughton, 1999, p. 192) developed in The Bronx, a borough of New York City, that came to be known as hip-hop. This new genre encompassed music (in DJ-ing and MC-ing), visual art (in graffiti) and dance (in b-boying/b-girling), as well as style, fashion and 'ideologies, performance and attitudes of mind' (Poschardt, 1998, p. 151). The term 'DJ-ing' is derived from an abbreviation of 'disc jockey', describing an individual who selects and plays pre-recorded material. The term MC-ing is derived from an abbreviation of 'master of ceremonies', describing an individual who introduces the DJ and keeps the crowd informed about occurrences during the hip-hop performance. Sometimes spelt 'emcee', this element of hip-hop culture is generally associated with what has become known as rapping.

By using only records, turntables and microphones, the musicians of early hip-hop culture created original music that, to many, sounded like a completely new musical language (Brewster and Broughton, 1999, p. 321). In order to compose music entirely from parts of other records, hip-hop DJs perfected incredible record manipulation skills. Malcolm McLaren reflected:

> It's using the debris of old music ... Finding little beats inside other people's records and mixing them together ... [it] doesn't follow the old fashioned format of verse-chorus ... That's what makes it one of the newest and the most interesting types of music being made today. (Taylor, 1998, p. 15)

By remaining in relative isolation throughout the culture's formative years, hip-hop music was free to develop without imposed boundaries. From 1973–1979 the fundamental elements of hip-hop music, including the appropriation and re-use of existing musical texts and the development of compositional processes, had all been established. In 1995 the term 'turntablism' emerged to reflect the artistic practices of the hip-hop DJ. The term was first used by DJ Babu of the Beat Junkies crew, who stated, 'My definition of a Turntablist is a person who uses the turntables not to play music, but to manipulate sound and create music' (Gragg, 1999). Although the term is not embraced by all hip-hop DJs and musicians, it is generally recognised and used within hip-hop culture. Within this context, a turntable team is a group of turntable musicians who come together to collectively compose and perform original music through the manipulation of records on turntables. Team members usually refer to the finished composition as a 'routine'.

A Chapter Outline

Chapter 1

Chapter 1 outlines the scope and content of the book, providing the rationale behind its production. The chapter outlines how this book offers a new approach to hip-hop scholarship as well as establishing the key contribution of the book as the development of an analytical methodology specifically for turntable music through the creation of a model framework for analysing compositional process supported by a new notation expressly for the analysis of turntable music. This chapter provides an overview of the book's content, briefly covering the historical and artistic context of the study, and goes on to provide a background to hip-hop turntablism and definitions of key terms, specifically hip-hop, turntablism, turntable teams and routines. This chapter also includes a description of the methodology of research and the different ways information was obtained from the different teams involved.

Chapter 2

Chapter 2 discusses the way in which creative collaboration has manifested itself within the different art forms of hip-hop as a whole. This sense of community and collectiveness is reflected in the collaborative creative practices of hip-hop, and this chapter will explore how hip-hop culture can not only be regarded as a way of life, but also as a way of creating, where individual artists work together to collectively create original art, in a range of different forms. This chapter will explore the different ways that collaboration has manifested itself within the creative processes of two other hip-hop art forms – dance (b-boying/b-girling) and visual arts (graffiti). Again, this discussion will focus on the artistic work itself.

Chapter 3

Chapter 3 explores the technological, artistic and cultural positioning of hip-hop team turntablism. It begins with a discussion of the history of the creative use of reproductive devices, focusing uniquely on an exploration of the creative uses that have culminated in the turntablists' relationship with the turntable. Rather than focusing on the technical discoveries and developments of recording technology, this historical overview will cover the *creative* uses of technology used in the late nineteenth and early twentieth centuries.

The chapter begins by establishing the turntable's early use as a creative rather than reproductive device, discussing the emerging technologies (both graphophone and gramophone) and their uses. The creative adoption of the new technologies is discussed, including reactions from contemporary musicians and theorists relating to its status as an instrument, the threats it posed to creativity and live performance and its potential as a new means of musical expression. The chapter provides a historical overview of turntable experimentation through two distinct histories – the work of DJs, from early radio pioneers to club DJs, and the field of experimental music and installation art. This section aims to explore both histories in terms of the creative use of the turntable, exploring the development of compositional strategies as well how the cultural tendencies of modernism and postmodernism are both evident in the routines of contemporary hip-hop turntablist teams. For this reason I will focus on the musical genres and artistic movements prior to hip-hop that reflect the turntable techniques of contemporary hip-hop teams, rather than an overview of DJ culture and turntable practice as a whole.

Chapter 4

Chapter 4 focuses on the contemporary practices of turntablism, covering the turntablists' relationship with the technology and the ways in which they have recoded and adapted the technology to suit their own technological and artistic needs. This includes discussion of key turntablist practitioners including the Scratch Perverts, Grandmaster Flash and DJ Theodore. The chapter discusses the way in which violations of technology became seen as a creative act borne out of a growing demand for instruments that met the needs of DJs, which in turn prompted the industry to develop instruments that met the requirements of turntable musicians.

The chapter continues with an overview of the equipment of the contemporary hip-hop turntablist. To overcome the difficulty of discussing such rapidly-developing music technology, this chapter refers to equipment through instrument type rather than specific models – turntables and mixer. It will, however, refer specifically to the Technics turntables, as they have remained the definitive hip-hop turntable for the past twenty years. The chapter concludes by outlining recent technological developments in DJ culture in the form of digital DJing systems, where a combination of software and hardware is replacing the traditional tools of the turntablist. This is followed by a discussion on how hip-hop turntablists are using this new technology and how these new tools may affect the creative practice of turntablism.

Chapter 5

Chapter 5 is the first of the chapters that looks specifically at the compositional processes of the turntable teams. It focuses on the main sound manipulation techniques used to create original sound material from records and discusses the implications of these in the development of new musical processes and practices. It does not aim to give detailed instructions about how the various techniques are executed as this information is already easily available in a wide range of instructional DJ books such as Brewster and Broughton's *How to DJ (Properly)* (2002). To look at these techniques in more detail they have been divided into three categories – structural techniques, rhythmic techniques, and melodic techniques. Each section will discuss specific techniques with reference to the turntable pioneers who invented and developed the techniques.

Chapter 6

Chapter 6 concerns the processes used by the hip-hop turntable teams to develop the new sonic material, created by manipulating the records, into an original composition. This chapter aims to explore particular notions of creative group work and ways in which these can be applied to the compositional processes of turntable teams. The early sections look at the formation and development of the teams in relation to established group work theories from the worlds of both business and the arts, then go on to explore notions of collaboration and devising, with specific reference to the creation of routines by the turntable teams the Scratch Perverts and the Mixologists. The chapter discusses the collective creation of turntable teams in relation to the process of devising, a process of collective creation used in contemporary dance and theatre. To be able to analyse the creative process of hip-hop turntable teams from a devising standpoint it is necessary to compare their creative processes with devising models and to assist in this, a model framework of the devising process has been constructed, through which to look at the creative processes of the turntable teams.

Chapter 7

Chapter 7 presents a suitable analytical methodology for the study of the compositional processes of hip-hop turntable teams and is structured in two sections. The first section looks at some existing analytical methodologies for hip-hop and popular music in general, discussing their suitability for an analysis of hip-hop team turntablism. Academic literature around the genre has tended to emerge from a variety of disciplines and many have been orientated towards a sociological or textual analysis, which results in an unbalanced analytical focus. To address the lack of academic work that deals with the actual music of hip-hop culture, this chapter will establish a methodology that values the creative process and supports its analysis rather than using a sociological analysis. The second section of this chapter focuses on frameworks for the analysis of hip-hop turntable music and the development of an analytical model. While it provides an analytical model that relates to a more formal analysis of music including elements such as tempo, form and instrumentation, it also facilitates a process-based analysis covering group organisation, sound manipulation techniques and creative process. Such a dual-focused approach offers a comprehensive framework through which to analyse team turntable composition.

Chapter 8

Chapter 8 explores the emerging notation and transcription techniques and, following a discussion of the implication and use of such systems, sets out a new notational system for the analysis of turntable team compositions. The last decade has witnessed a significant development of notation and transcription techniques within turntable music, which are useful for the analysis of turntable music. This chapter outlines and discusses a number of approaches to turntable notation that have evolved to date and goes on to identify five main functions of turntables, discussing how the different schools of turntable notation reflect the different intentions of the users.

The existing turntable transcription techniques are adequate when notating either for purposes of documentation or communication between musicians. However, any one of the approaches alone is not sufficient for a full analysis of team turntablism and so the chapter concludes with outlining a new transcription method based on aspects of the existing systems. This method will aim to encompass material, manipulation techniques and structure as well as tempo, timescale and the roles of individual musicians. Through using the transcription system, anyone undertaking an analysis of turntable composition is able to establish the structure of the composition in relation to sound generation and sound manipulation techniques, isolate sonic and rhythmic patterns and track their development throughout the work and identify tempo and timescale and the roles of individual musicians within the composition.

Chapter 9

Chapter 9 contains the bulk of the analysis and discusses and analyses two hip-hop turntable routines in turn, the Scratch Perverts' routine performed at the DJ Team Championships in 1999 and the Mixologists' routine performed at the DMC World Team Championships in 2001. Through the analysis, the chapter determines the collaborative processes and techniques used in the creation of team turntable routines, and establishes characteristics of hip-hop team turntable compositions.

To gain the best possible insight into such processes, the analysis of each routine is split into two main parts. The first discusses the process of collective creation in relation to the devising framework as established in Chapter 5, and the second analyses the completed routine through the analytical framework established in Chapter 6.

Following the analysis of both the creative process and the resulting artistic product, the chapter concludes with a comparison of the three routines, establishing in depth a number of characteristics of team turntable composition.

Chapter 10

The conclusion pulls together the content of the preceding eight chapters, drawing together the central points, arguments and findings of the book.

Chapter 2
Hip-Hop and Collaboration

From its outset in the 1970s, hip-hop was not solely a musical genre, but encompassed dance (b-boying/b-girling) and visual art (graffiti). According to Schloss (2009) these art-based forms of early hip-hop shared an aesthetic sensibility (p. 4), individuals moving between different interest groups and forms of expression, leading to a cross-pollination of art forms (p. 83). He describes hip-hop as an practice taught and performed through face to face interactions, quoting Anthony Colon, b-boy and graffiti artist who comments; '… the main thing is that hip-hop, breaking, graffiti is about the people' (p. 40). Similarly, Greg Dimitriadis (2004) reflects how early hip-hop was characterised by integrated practices – an aesthetic integration supported and developed through interaction and communication (pp. 421–2). Early hip-hop, he contests, remained a 'function of live practice and congregation', dependent on face-to-face social contact (p. 421). Colon describes how the community aspect was central across the hip-hop art forms:

> … everything that started coming out at that time, you did it together … Whether you did the graffiti, the bombing, you did it together. You went together …
> (Schloss, 2009, p. 54)

Hip-hop culture is more than just a collection of art forms; it is a way of life, a culture in a much deeper sense, encompassing 'ideologies … and attitudes of mind' (Poschardt, 1998, p. 151) as well as 'an empowering identity, a behaviour, an attitude …' (KRS-One, 2003, p. 211). From its outset, hip-hop has been defined by notions of community and creative collaboration. In his book *Ruminations,* KRS-One (a significant figure in the hip-hop community), describes hip-hop as a 'collective behaviour' (2003, p. 180) established as 'a community of peace, love unity and having fun … an independent and unique community, an empowering behaviour, and an international culture' (2003, p. 179). Hip-hop he contests, 'was (and still is) the collective consciousness that created and expressed Rap music, Graffiti art and Break dancing.' (2003, p. 181). According to Jeff Chang in *Total Chaos – The Art and Aesthetics of Hip-Hop* (2007), hip-hop is 'a grand expression of our collective creative powers' (p. x). KRS-One refers to the 'collective creativity' within hip-hop (p. 191). How is this sense of community and collectiveness reflected in the collaborative creative practices of hip-hop? Could this integration extend to creative practices, making hip-hop an inherently collaborative creative genre?

B-boying

Community

In b-boying culture, a group of b-boys or b-girls who dance and battle together are referred to as a crew. A 'battle' is a competitive dance-off between individual dancers or crews (DJ Hooch, 2011, p. 20). Joseph Schloss focuses on the work of New York b-boys and b-girls, discussing the principles and strategies of b-boy performance and the creative cooperation of battling teams, who 'use style to reconcile opposing forces' (in Chang, 2007, p. 27). Community is central to b-boying and b-girling. B-boying is learnt through personal interaction (Schloss, 2009, p. 40) and the foundation of boy-boying/b-girling is passed on from generation to generation, teacher to student through a kind of apprenticeship system (Schloss, 2009, p. 51):

> ... the way the dance is taught exerts a profound influence on the way it is experienced. It affects the way individuals understand the history of the form and their place in it, the way they express their individual and group identities and the way they pass this knowledge onto others. (Schloss, 2009, p. 41)

The importance of this is reflected in the feelings of practitioners, b-boy FLOWREXsac (2012) reflecting:

> The community aspect relates to hip hop as a movement and a culture and without it, what is the point of practicing, training and learning these arts if we can't exchange, compare or influence or be influenced and taught by others? We all push each others' projects and have fought to be recognised in the professional arts scene in order to create opportunities to enable artists to train and perform as a viable means to live the culture working together and promoting what we are doing as a whole scene.

B-Girl Emiko explains how crews are strengthened by the ties of friendship:

> Crews should just be the people who [you] always hung out with ... You go there, battle together, and maybe after the battle together you do eat together ... that's the way it should be. That way, when battle comes, it will be tighter. (Schloss, 2009, p. 56)

The b-boys and b-girls draw parallels between the groups and family. When describing how he was put into a crew, B-boy Crazy Legs comments:

... it was all about family: it was about bringing people together ... from situations without any kind of social activity, to be involved in this. It brought us all together in a way that made us feel good about what we were doing. (DJ Hooch, 2011, p. 7)

FLOWREXsac reflects how this familial nature results in a strength that supports crew battles:

From a crew standpoint a crew should be an army of people fighting for each other in battle, a crew should be about family and unity, one of the best experiences you can enjoy is being part of a strong crew or crew who want to hang out with each other not just in training for at the jams but actually contribute to each others' lives as friends and family ... Crew is family. This translates when you see crews who are family in battle, cohesion and teamwork seem to be important factors in winning crew battles it is always easy to spot a bunch of high level dancers who have been put together for one jam but don't actually know each other.

Javier Reyes (hip-hop actor and writer, and co-founder and Artistic Director of American theatre company Colored Ink) correlates hip-hop theatre to a family reunion, describing how '... everyone starts vibing off each other and contributing bits and pieces of each other to make something new ...' (in Chang, 2007, p. 81).

Creating Routines

Through practicing together in crews the individual b-boy/b-girl is pushed to develop their skills. Teknyk (a member of the USA crew Skillmethodz, World Champion Crew, 2003) describes how a crew is a driving source for continual improvement, reflecting, 'We feed off each other and push each other to strive to continue to be better day in and day out' (DJ Hooch, 2011, p. 116). Venum (a member of the USA crew Skillmethodz, World Champion Crew, 2009), reinforces the idea of this positive creative environment:

We are some of the best and most innovative at what we do in the world, and we are that way because of each other. We believe in each other's talents and constantly push each other to grow and get better. Having a crew gives you a sense of brotherhood and support that you'd never have solo. I am blessed with ... being in a place that I am able to give back to my community. (DJ Hooch, 2011, p. 134)

Schloss reflects on the interplay between the individual b-boy/b-girl and their place in the crew:

> ... the standardisation of the form allows each individual's story to be connected with all the others. This gives rise to a rich ... social mosaic where each individuals' expression also contributes to the beauty of the collective. (Schloss, 2009, p. 92)

B-boy Storm describes how in his crew, the German group Animatronik, collective work in creating routines is a conscious process, explaining how, 'from diagnosing what we do this dance, to the architecture of the counter move, in this group we practice, test, analyse and theorize ...' (DJ Hooch, 2011, p. 148). During crew battles, crews can move between improvised individual movement and pre-planned group choreography:

> The transitions are not merely a matter of smooth choreography, but also bring into play such things as what the collective vision will be for the routines, how the individual expressions will relate to that collective vision and how confidently the two can be brought together. (Schloss, 2009, p. 55)

Schloss likens the way in which crews move between improvised and choreographed movement to the way jazz musicians move from between being part of the ensemble to being the soloist, describing how, 'part of the movement through time involves negotiating opportunities to shift from organised group expression to improvised individual statements ...' (2009, p. 55). FLOWREXsac explains how these choreographed crew can be a powerful tool in battle:

> ... on the world stage of competition you will undoubtedly come across situations where an opponent crew will bring a big routine out, not having one or two may seem like you are unprepared or not able to answer back.

Graffiti

Community

According to Janice Rahn in *Painting without Permission* (2002), graffiti is rooted in community and collaboration (p. 162), and it is regarded by Imuris Valle and Eduardo Weiss (2009) as 'a community of support' (p. 134). From the mid-1970s, crews have been formed by graffiti artists to offer what Richard S. Christen (2003, p. 71) describes as '... collaboration and support' – loose associations of graffiti artists who come together to paint together and to battle (Rahn, 2002, p. 5). Valle and Weiss describe the term as referring to 'teamwork and cooperation aimed at a common goal' (p. 130). Graffiti crews can include between 2–200 people

(Docuyanan, 2000, p. 108) and produce individual as well as group work. Artists may belong to more than one crew simultaneously (Valle and Weiss, 2010, p. 131).

Christen outlines a number of structured stages that graffiti artists would move through, the second of which involves the creative collaboration inherent in the crews, developing close relationships with other crew members (2003, p. 62). Valle and Weiss regard Graffiti Crews as communities of practice, artists interacting face-to-face (p. 129) and learning their art through observation and practice (p. 130). The authors discuss how graffiti artists form these communities, referring to Wenger's definition of communities of practice (2008) that includes aspects relevant to collaboration – 'they share a passion', 'they are defined by this shared area of interest', 'they engage in joint activities', 'they share information', 'they build relationships', and they develop 'a shared practice' (p. 134).

Creating Artwork

Valle and Weiss describe how group projects are planned and carried out within crews, artists pooling money for resources and painting together. During such group projects, tasks are assigned according to level of experience. Novices may locate good painting spaces, and other members fill in the outlines created by the most experienced artists (2010, p. 130). Emmett G. Price (2006, p. 31) describes how in the early 1970s, graffiti artists formed into guilds, including the United Graffiti Artists (UGA) and the Nation of Graffiti Artists (NOGA). Indeed, Christen describes how some crews were modelled like medieval guilds, the less experienced artists doing simpler painting tasks for those with greater expertise, as in some kind of apprenticeship. While the crew works together to create the new artwork they may talk about the techniques they are using, their choice of paint, or other work they have seen, a practice identified by Valle and Weiss as supporting 'communal forms of memory and reflection, as well as to signal membership' (2010, pp. 130–31).

Citing Maffesoli's work on 'tribes' of young people (1990), Valle and Weiss reflect how the levels of interaction and emotion evident in such groups of young people aids the process of creation (Valle and Weiss, p. 131):

> Graffiti artists share the emotion of painting, of vibrating together in their adventures and in their memories. In this sense, graffiti artists could be fully described as a "tribe" in post-modern culture. Predominant in this tribe is the "aesthetic aura" along with aesthetic/sense-based experiences and entertaining activities. Yet being and vibrating together is not limited to emotions; it also implies work and skill. (p. 133)

Christen describes how crew members support each other by collaborating on pieces, but comments how members also battle within the crew, pushing each other 'to higher levels of creativity and achievement' (p. 73). Graffiti artist EAZ ONE regards collaboration as a motivator:

> You know it's different if you have people tagging or bombing *with* you. You
> push each other as opposed to trying to come out of the box yourself. 'Cause
> then you have no drive. It's just really hard, especially if you are young. (Rahn,
> 2002, p. 188)

This is reflected in the thoughts of Graffiti artist DSTRBO:

> The whole point of PUZZLE was collaboration, making one piece with two
> people. Seeing that dynamic would produce something neither of us would have
> produced on our own. (Rahn, 2002, p. 155)

While competition is at the heart of hip-hop (Toop, 2000, p. 15) so, I would
suggest, is collaboration and cooperation. Mentoring, for example, is evident
in the forms of hip-hop discussed above, and, as Schloss states, 'understanding
the values implicit in these relationships can provide important insights into the
cultural values of hip-hop' (2009, p. 67). Emmett G Price talks of a 'Hip Hop
aesthetic' that holds together the different elements of hip-hop (2006, p. 40), 'each
in its own way representing a passion for life and a commitment to individual
and collective expression (p. 41). Danny Hoch (2007, pp. 354–5) identifies 14
aesthetic elements that he feels characterise hip-hop's original four elements:
Codification of language, Call-and-response, Sociopolitical context and legacy,
Metaphor and Simile, Illusion, Polyculturalism, Battle, Lack of safety, barriers,
boundaries, African- and Caribbean-diaspora performing traditions, Lack of
resources and access, Reappropriation, Urban blight, Criminalization of poverty
and Criminalization of culture. Hoch suggests that hips-hop's aesthetics 'lie
foremost in the social context from which it sprung' (p. 350). I would suggest then
that collective creation and creative collaboration, manifested within the different
art forms of hip-hop, are also part of the hip-hop aesthetic.

Chapter 3
Turntablism in Context

The History of the Creative Use of Reproductive Devices

In the composition work of hip-hop turntablist teams, the turntable becomes a musical instrument with which to create and perform original pieces of music. This chapter aims to explore the history of the creative use of an instrument that at its inception was envisaged as a piece of reproductive apparatus. The section will not focus on the technical discoveries and developments of recording technology, nor on the detailed workings of these machines, but will instead explore their creative uses that have culminated in the turntablists' relationship with the turntable and the 'musical revolution' (Poschardt, 1998, p. 15) that this relationship brought about.

The creative use of reproductive technology was established early in the development of the equipment. As early as the mid-to-late 1800s, purchasers of cylinder phonographs and graphophones were using the equipment not only to listen to pre-recorded music, but also to make their own vocal and instrumental recordings. Both Edison's phonograph and Bell-Tainter's graphophone offered sound recording and playback, using wax as a recording medium to allow the recording to be removed from the cylinder and stored for later listening. Edison's Standard, Home and Triumph cylinder phonographs incorporated a shaver to erase previously recorded impressions. Chew (1967) regards the possibility of home recording that both the phonograph and graphophone offered as being the chief selling point of the cylinder machines. Although Edison's primary application for his machine was telephony, Goodall (2001) cites how in 1878 Edison outlined nine other uses for the phonograph, only one of which was related to music. These nine uses were office dictation and letter writing, talking books for the visually impaired, teaching of proper elocution, reproduction of music, archiving family sayings, toys, speaking clocks, preservation of endangered languages and distance learning. While these purposes demonstrate no potential creative *musical* use of the gramophone, restricting it to reproduction, it is evident that a *general* creative use of the phonograph was anticipated even at this early stage of the turntable's development. This is apparent through both the home recording potential of the machine and the user's relationship with the technology. The archiving of family sayings, for example, can be regarded as a creative use of the phonograph as it allows groups or individual users to plan and execute their own home recordings to play back later at their discretion. Indeed, promotional material released to advertise the Edison-Bell phonograph highlights this creative use of the technology:

> At your home, by the fireside, suitable for cottage or Mansion. It is a singer, a reciter, a piano, cornet, clarionette, piccolo, or any other instrument. Will faithfully record and reproduce any sound that is or ever can be produced ... You can make your own Records and take and immediately reproduce those of your friends and children, whether vocal or instrumental. (Ord-Hume, 1973, p. 284)

Even the uses outlined by Edison that do not refer to the domestic creation of new recordings, for example office dictation, elocution or distance learning, tend towards the user having an active rather than a passive relationship with the technology.

Although Edison did not envisage the creative and commercial potential of his invention (Goodall, 2001, p. 185), the first manipulation of recorded sound for the purpose of entertainment took place using the phonograph. Seventy years before the DJs who would use record manipulation to create and perform pieces of music, travelling showmen would, as the grand finale to an evening's entertainment, instantly record a cornettist and then perform a speeded-up version of the recording by turning the phonograph handle faster and faster. As Chew (1967) comments, from 1890 onwards it was becoming increasingly clear that this equipment had potential for both home entertainment and public amusements. In a similar way to the relationship between contemporary turntablist musicians and the music technology manufacturers, the demand for music from the public and the developments in technology necessary to meet this need spurred the industry into action.

The promotional literature for the New Columbia graphophone stressed that the machines were, 'Not a cheap toy, but a well made instrument' (Ord-Hume, 1973, p. 283). However, professional musicians were not yet using the technology creatively and their professional relationship with the machines extended only to recording musical works to be sold commercially. Goodall describes how many classical musicians were suspicious of the new technology, citing Sir Arthur Sullivan:

> I am astonished and somewhat terrified. Astonished at the wonderful power you have developed and terrified at the thought that so much hideous and bad music may be put on record for ever. (Goodall, 2001, p. 188)

In 1895, a commercial version of Emile Berliner's flat disc gramophone was introduced and was in production by the end of the century. The gramophone soon overtook the phonograph and graphophone in terms of popularity as the recordings, on disc rather than cylinder, made longer, better quality recordings possible. Although this new machine was regarded as a musical instrument by 'the man in the street' (Chew, 1967, p. 50), the gramophone did not offer home-recording technology and so was restricted to playing the records that were commercially available. Indeed, until the introduction of relatively cheap home lathes over 100 years later, the creative use of the gramophone through home recording was impossible. However, although using the gramophone as a recording device was no longer an option, musicians looking for other creative outlets for recording technology began to experiment with the gramophone and later turntable technology as a performing and composing device.

Although some creative use of recording technology had been envisaged at the outset, the full creative impact of the turntable came not from home recording, but from what Poschardt regards as, 'an act of courageous and autonomous redefinition' (1998, p. 359). Musicians from many musical genres began to experiment with the creative potential of the turntable, transforming it from a reproductive device to a musical instrument, simultaneously transforming our relationship to music (Coleman, 2003). The struggle between format and function that Coleman regards as characteristic of nineteenth century recording technology was set to continue in the twentieth. In 1911, Felix Auerbach, cited in Rudolph Lothar (1924), questioned the status of the gramophone as a musical instrument, regarding it as one of the great, 'aberrations in the art-business':

> Concerning the realm of music, it is difficult to decide whether to give the gramophone a place among musical instruments; indeed, it is quite dubious whether it will ever win such a status. (Rudolph Lothar, 1924, p. 56)

Similarly, in his 1934 article 'The Form of the Record', Theodor Adorno sets out his argument concerning the negative effects of the record, which he regards as being 'the complete adversary of that which is human and artistic' (in Block and Glasmeier, 1989, p. 49). Adorno warns that the record may have a damaging effect on musical creativity, contributing nothing to artistic form and robbing music of 'living production' and goes as far as to suggest that it threatens the life of the art work itself (ibid., p. 50). According to Sérgio Freire (2003), in his article 'Early Musical Impressions from Both Sides of the Loudspeaker', the invention of the gramophone did not immediately result in either a sudden change in musical discourse or new artistic modes. Some composers, however, did search for a more creative relationship with the gramophone that would develop new means of musical expression. In 1926 for example, during the festival of chamber music in Donaueschingen, the suggestion was made to use the record as a creative medium of its own (Block and Glasmeier, p. 265) and Stravinsky considered the possibility of 'creating specific music for phonographic reproduction, music that would get its true image, that of the original sound, through mechanical reproduction' (cited in Glasmeier, 1989, p. 30). Mark Katz, in his book *Capturing Sound* (2005), cites Hansjörg Dammert, composer and pupil of Arnold Schoenberg, who in 1926 called for a new kind of concert music – a 'concerto for phonograph' where the phonograph would take the part of the solo instrument, accompanied by live orchestra (Dammert, 1926, p. 406) and works of both Ottorina Respighi (*Pines of Rome* of 1924) and Kurt Weill (*Der Zar lässt sich photographieren* of 1927), both include sound played from a phonograph, without manipulation (Katz, 2005, p.108).

One of the most creative uses of the gramophone or phonograph, however, was to be found not in writing music specifically *for* record but *with* records. John Cage, quoted by Hans Rudolf Zeller (1989), in his article 'Media Composition According to Cage', encouraged the creative use of records in the making of new and original music:

> ... though people think they can use records as music, what they have to finally understand is, that they have to use them as records. And music instructs us, I would say, that the uses of things, if they are meaningful, are creative; therefore the only lively thing that will happen with a record, is, if somehow you would use it to make something which it isn't. If you could for instance make another piece of music with a record ... that I would find interesting ... But unfortunately most people who collect records and use them, use them in quite another way. They use them as a kind of portable museum or portable concert-hall. (Reproduced in Block and Glasmeier, p. 73)

A Historical Overview of Turntable Experimentation

The background to the creative musical use of the turntable falls into two distinct histories. The most well known of these relates to the work of DJs, from early radio pioneers to club DJs. The other earlier, equally important history, lies outside popular music in the field of experimental music and installation art. This section aims to explore both histories in terms of the creative use of the turntable, exploring the development of compositional strategies as well as how the cultural tendencies of modernism and postmodernism are both evident in the routines of contemporary hip-hop turntablist teams. For this reason the discussion will focus on the musical genres and artistic movements prior to hip-hop that reflect the turntable techniques of contemporary hip- hop teams, rather than an overview of DJ culture and turntable practice as a whole.

Experimental Music and Installation Art and the Development of
Sound Manipulation Techniques in the 1920s–1980s

Turntable experimentation and the development of turntable-based sound manipulation techniques also occurred outside popular music, in the fields of experimental music and installation art. These musicians were not united by any one artistic movement or concept but rather by their desire to experiment with the creative potential of the turntable for their own compositional end. In the early part of the twentieth century some composers became interested in the creative potential of the phonograph or gramophone, undertaking small-scale experiments and explorations. During the 1920s, Paul Hindemith, Ernst Toch and Percy Grainger each observed the subjective effects of playing records at different speeds (Manning, 2003, p. 5). Between 1922 and 1927 Darius Milhaud experimented with transforming recordings of voices using speed variation and in 1930 Paul Hindemith and Ernst Toch explored the timbral and textural possibilities of the phonograph, performing compositions incorporating pre-recorded discs. Hindemith's *Trickaufnahmen* (trick recordings) investigated the technical abilities of the instrument as well as the performer, exploring a range of sound manipulation techniques including acceleration and deceleration of discs and the pitch changes this causes, experimenting with timbre and texture (Katz, 2005, p. 100). Katz suggests that Hindemith performed his compositions using two phonographs simultaneously. In 1936, Edgar Varèse also experimented with record manipulation, playing records backwards at a variety of speeds (Block and Glasmeier, p. 266). Although many of these experiments were undertaken on an individual basis, in 1928 the Hochschule für Musik in Berlin facilitated a research programme in the manipulation of phonographic records that involved both Hindemith and Toch (Manning, 2003, p. 9).

Between 1930 and 1980, four major turntable pioneers emerged from a range of musical and artistic backgrounds; two primarily visual artists (Lázló Moholy-Nagy and Christian Marclay) and two composers (Pierre Schaeffer and John Cage). The sound manipulation techniques of these artists fall into two categories; techniques that affect the physical properties of the record itself and techniques that use the turntable.

Manipulation Techniques that Affect the Physical Properties of the Record

A number of the turntable composers manipulated the sound on the record, prior to being placed on the turntable. During the 1930s, Lázló Moholy–Nagy, Oskar Fischinger and Paul Arma attempted to alter the acoustic content of records before amplification by carving graphic structures into gramophone records and running the record backwards against the stylus to scratch new patterns. (Poschardt, 1998, p. 349) For Moholy-Nagy, the gramophone is a basis for production not reproduction:

> As production (productive creation) above all serves the human condition, we attempt to further our purposes of creative production through the uses of those apparatuses (methods) which until now, have been used only for reproduction purposes. (Moholy-Nagy, 1967, p. 28, cited in Glasmeier, 1989, p. 28)

He hoped that his experiments with turntable music would result in the creation of a new musical language, a 'groove-script ABC', through studying the graphic signs on the record:

> The graphic signs allow us to establish a new graphic-mechanical scale, which is to say a new mechanical harmony, by examining the individual graphic signs and bringing their relationships into a law. (Block and Glasmeier, p. 53)

Maholy-Nagy's system would enable the composer to create the composition directly on the record, ready for reproduction without the need for a performer. Music creation would become independent from major orchestral enterprises and all other instruments would be redundant. For Moholy-Nagy this greatly democratised music creation:

> Instead of producing the many "reproduction-talents" who are neither actively or passively involved in real sound form, people will be trained to be true music receivers or creators. (In Moholy-Nagy's 1923 article 'New Plasticism in Music: Possibilities of the Gramophone', reprinted in Block and Glasmeier, p. 56)

This concept of the record as basis for production is also evident in the turntable music of Christian Marclay, for example in the composition *John Cage* which is a recording of a collage made by cutting slices from a number of records and gluing them together to form a single disc. His record *Footsteps* also explores the effects of physically altering the record – 3,500 records were used as flooring at an art exhibition over six weeks, packed in individual covers and then sold. For Marclay, such experiments that alter and distort the original recording highlight his understanding of the record as a constantly changing 'capsule of sound' and he deliberately brings the residual sounds of pops, clicks and scratches to the foreground of the composition.

Manipulation Techniques Using the Turntable

One of the earliest examples of manipulating records using the turntable is a 1920 Dada performance, where eight phonograph performers played classical and popular discs simultaneously, playing them forward, in reverse and at different speeds (Katz, 2005, p. 108). In 1930, Toch composed and performed *Gesprochene Musik*, which used specially recorded discs of spoken text, commenting how '… in exploiting the mechanical possibilities of recording (such as increasing tempo and therefore pitch), a kind of instrumental music came about, so that it maybe perhaps nearly forgotten that its creation is based solely on speech' (1930, pp. 221–2, in Katz, 2005).

Pierre Schaeffer's formative work in musique concrète also involved the manipulation of recordings using gramophones using originally recorded material. In his treatise 'Esquisse d'un Solfège Concret' (1952), Schaeffer sets out his methods of both sonic manipulation and construction. He lists three methods of sound manipulation prior to composition, including *transmutation,* manipulation of material without altering the form; *transformation*, manipulation of form without altering the material; and *modulation*, neither transmutation nor transformation, but variation applied to either pitch, intensity or timbre. Schaeffer goes on to highlight structural processes which he refers to as *Preparations*, the use of classical, exotic or modern musical instruments as sound sources without restriction as to mode of performance; *Montage*, construction by the simple juxtaposition of pre-recorded fragments; and *Mixage*, the superimposition of monophonies to create polyphonic textures. Manning (2003) describes how Schaeffer's possibilities were limited to four manipulation techniques; playing records backwards and forwards, juxtaposing sounds taken from their original time continuum; playing recordings at different speeds and creating repetitive sound loops by breaking the groove at specific points. Many turntable composers manipulate the sound of records by creating repeating loops or 'locked grooves'. Schaeffer was the first to use this technique, pressing records with a groove that holds the stylus in a continuous cycle, looping the sound as the record rotates. This technique was used in *Etude aux Chemins de Fer* (1948) which was constructed from successive extracts of material made from manipulated recordings of steam locomotives at Gare des Batignolles, Paris. For Schaeffer, the use of loops in composition posed problems associated with the repetitive nature of the material. In attempting to achieve continuity in his compositions through the careful choice and use of manipulated recordings of traditional instruments, Schaeffer found himself faced with the difficulty of creating something new from a recognisable sound source. Even after manipulation, he felt that the sound sources were still identifiable, leading to what he regarded as problems of association. For Schaeffer, the basic manipulation techniques available to him – looping, reversing and altering speed – did not produce the originality of sound that he desired. *Etude aux Tourniquets* (1948) introduced new sonorities into his compositions through the use of manipulated sound recordings of toys and percussion instruments, but the origins of the sounds are still clear. Schaeffer deliberately excluded any techniques that directly altered the physical content of the recordings (Manning, 2003, p. 6) and his primary technique was based on juxtaposing the manipulated elements to create 'new perspectives regarding association and contrast' (ibid., p. 7).

Cage also used turntable manipulation techniques in his compositions. In his *Imaginary Landscape No. 1* (1939) for example, the records alternate between two speeds – 33 and 78 rpm and rhythms are created through lifting and lowering the record needle onto the record. In 'For More New Sounds', Cage describes the variety of manipulation techniques that were used in the composition:

> Frequency records and the recording of the whine of a generator were used on turntables, the speed of which could be varied, thus making sliding tones available. To produce the sound, a needle was lowered to the record, although this sometimes resulted in a blurred attack. A button arrangement was preferred, whereby it was possible to have the needle on the record before a required entrance, sound or silence being produced by the position of the button. Here again, the loudness of the sound could be controlled very exactly. One player can operate several turntables and perform a single line written for the sound of a landslide, that of rain, of compressed air, or any other recorded sounds. (In Kostelanetz (ed.) 1970, p. 65)

Cage also composed other works involving the creative use of turntable technology. In *Credo in Us* (1942) the player of the phonograph is instructed, 'If phonograph, use some classic, for e.g. Dvorak, Beethoven, Sibelius or Schostakovich' (Block and Glasmeier, p. 266). *Imaginary Landscape No. 5* (1952) was composed for 42 records and *33 1/3* (1969) for 12 record players. This creative use of turntable technology also extended to the phonograph itself. In *Cartridge Music* (1960), performers are directed to amplify small sounds using pick-ups taken from the tone arms of record players.

The DJs' Creative Use of the Turntable and the Development of
Sound Manipulation Techniques in the 1940s–1980s

The 1970s and early 1980s witnessed a club-based popular music revolution that developed and established what Brewster and Broughton (1999) regard as 'some of the most radical innovations to date in the way music is envisaged, created and consumed' (p. 123) and took DJs from using one turntable, to two and sometimes three decks. These innovations, taking place as they did on turntables, established the concept of the DJ as music creator rather than solely player of records and paved the way for the sound manipulation techniques and compositional processes of hip-hop turntablist musicians. Although these innovations developed from within radio stations and then club culture, they were not limited to specific musical styles or location, but rather developed out of a shared desire to be the best DJ and create and manipulate the best club night possible.

Coleman charts the history of the Disc Jockey in three distinct phases – commercial innovators (1948–1965), musical innovators (1965–1979) and technological innovators (1973 to the present day) (2003, pp. xii–xiii). However, in the study of DJs' development of sound manipulation and compositional techniques, such a clear-cut distinction is not possible. Radio DJs for example, regarded by Coleman as 'commercial innovators' for the way in which they influenced and exploited musical taste for commercial gain, played an important part in the development of turntable techniques. In order to enhance his promotions of certain records for example, Bill Curtis (veteran DJ for American station WUFO) began to manipulate the records he played, extending the record through a mixture of slowing down, repeating and talking over the track. In the 1970s, DJ Francis Grasso introduced into club DJing the fundamental technique of slip-cueing that he had learnt from friends working as radio DJs (Brewster and Broughton, 1999, p. 131). Slip-cueing requires the DJ to place a felt mat between the turntable and the platter holding the record stationary whilst the turntable continues moving underneath, allowing the record to immediately spin in time when it is dropped into the mix. Many radio DJs had soon evolved beyond the 'characterless gramophone technician' (ibid., p. 31) and helped to develop a number of major turntable techniques, including mixing, rewinding, cutting and pasting.

Mixing

The first DJ to introduce the fundamental turntable technique of mixing was Terry Noel, resident DJ at the 1960s New York nightclub *Arthur*. Although working with a relatively simple set-up, having only a volume dial for each turntable, Noel subtly mixed tracks in a way never heard before:

> People would come up to me and say, "I was listening to the Mamas and the Papas and now I'm listening to the Stones and I didn't even know." I used to try some of the widest changes without losing a beat. (Brewster and Broughton, 1999, p. 63)

Poschardt (1998) names the first club DJ to manipulate recorded material for artistic purposes as Francis Grasso, Disco DJ at *The Sanctuary* in New York. Perhaps no coincidence, Grasso began DJing in 1968 by taking over from Noel at *Salvation Too* nightclub. Prior to Grasso's turntable experiments, DJs played records one at a time, treating each as 'discrete performances' (ibid., p. 127) and club evenings lacked a cohesive flow due to the constant start-stop of three-minute records. Although Grasso was not the first DJ to mix two records together, he was the first to deliberately perfect beat mixing as a creative DJ technique commenting, 'Nobody had really kept the beat going ... They'd get them to dance, then change records, so you had to catch the beat again. It never flowed' (ibid., p. 126). The development of mixing techniques were not helped by what was, by today's standards, very basic turntable technology. Early beat mixing was a high precision technique due to the lack of speed adjustment on the turntables, requiring the DJ to start the record at exactly the right moment. Grasso's mixing technique was so developed he would sometimes undertake his manipulations by eye rather then ear, recognising the required section of record from the grooves on the disc (ibid., p. 132). These techniques had four musical purposes; to overlay two different tracks, to create a seamless transition that would not interrupt the dynamic of the dance floor, to extend the length of a track or to create echo effects. Many of these skills were developed from necessity. As records only lasted for around three minutes, they needed to be extended to fulfil the needs of the dance floor.

Grasso's manipulation techniques took him from being a record selector and player to the position of a visionary creator, Brewster and Broughton regarding him as the first DJ to present a truly creative performance (ibid., p. 123). Before him, many DJs viewed records as separate musical entities, but the possibilities offered by Grasso's beat mixing enabled tracks to be seen as 'continuous elements' within a larger structure (ibid., p. 127):

> He was the first to show that a nightful of records could be a single thing: a
> voyage, a narrative, a set ... only after him did the DJ recognise that (this) power
> belonged to him, not to the records. (Ibid., p. 125)

Francis Grasso used his mixing techniques to create seamless musical soundtracks,
sometimes playing a copy of the same record on each turntable, explaining in an
interview with Brewster and Broughton how he used his manipulation techniques
to construct the extended version of Little Sister's *You're the One*:

> Part one ended musically, part two on the other side would begin with a scream,
> so you could blend right into the scream side, and then go back to "You're the
> One". Or play the scream side twice, part two, then flip it over and play part one,
> twice. (Ibid., p. 132)

Other nightclub DJs were also involved in the development of turntable
techniques. At the nightclub Paradise Garage, DJ Larry Levan perfected the
practice of constructing music from many different sources, blending rock, pop
electronica, soul, rap, funk and disco. As he describes in Brewster and Broughton,
'I found myself taking things from here, from there ... and using lots of things as
a base to take things from' (ibid., p. 262). In a similar vein Frankie Knuckles, DJ
at the Warehouse, incorporated sound effects into his sets. In an unconscious nod
to Pierre Schaeffer's *Etude aux Chemin de Fer*, Knuckles played an extended
sound effect of a speeding steam train, panning the sound from the front to the
back of the club, giving the effect of a train ploughing through the dance floor
(ibid., p. 271).

Rewinding, Cutting and Pasting

In 1950s and 1960s Jamaica, Reggae musicians began a radical relationship
with their records that changed the status of records through the transformation
of recorded music into a live event, and as such is central to the music of
contemporary turntablist teams (ibid., p. 105). Coleman comments how until 1995
Jamaica had no music copyright laws and Reggae DJs used records for their own
creative ends. Through manipulation techniques including EQ alterations, adding
effects and vocals as well as pioneering tricks such as the 'rewind' (spinning back
a record to be repeated) the DJs made original compositions based on rhythm
tracks from popular records. As Coleman reflects, 'No one owns a song or melody
or rhythm; music makers simply borrow tunes, returning them in slightly different
form' (Coleman, 2003, p. 136). For Reggae musicians the record was no longer
appreciated as a finished product, but as a 'tool of composition for a grander
performance' (Brewster and Broughton, 1999, p. 136).

In the early 1970s, disco DJ Walter Gibbons undertook innovations in sound
manipulation techniques during his time at the club Galaxy 21. Gibbons developed
turntable-based cut and paste techniques to manipulate small sections of drum

breaks, the forerunner to the beat-juggling techniques used by contemporary turntablist musicians:

> Everything he was doing back then, people are doing now. He was phasing records – playing two records at the same time to give a flange effect – and doubling up records so that there would be a little repeat. He would do tremendous quick cuts on records, sort of like b-boys do. He would slam it on so quick that you couldn't hear the turntable slowing down or catching up. (Jellybean Benitez in ibid., p. 152)

Walter Gibbons' cut and paste manipulation techniques enabled him to construct small sections of music into an original whole at the turntable. François Kevorkian, a drummer who worked with Gibbons, described how the DJ was so technically adept his manipulation techniques would often go unnoticed:

> Walter had an amazing instinct for drum breaks ... Creating drama with little bits of records, just like a hip-hop DJ, but he was incredibly fast at cutting up records. So smooth and seamless that you couldn't even tell that he was mixing records. You thought the version he played was actually on the record, but in fact he was taking little 10-second pieces. (Ibid., p. 153)

(Post)Modernism and Hip-Hop Turntablist Teams

As well as establishing the creative use of the turntable and the development of turntable-specific manipulation techniques, these earlier turntable pioneers also reflected certain modernist, and in some cases postmodernist tendencies. It will be demonstrated that contemporary hip-hop turntable teams seem to acknowledge these tendencies established by their predecessors whether consciously or not. Very simply stated, the turntable work of Moholy-Nagy and Schaeffer in the 1930s and 1940s displays characteristics of a modernist approach in the great importance their work placed on progress and innovation. Although they used records to create original compositions these were made specifically for the purpose. In both Cage and Marclay's work with turntables, a postmodern approach can also be detected. Both composers appropriated existing records and used these in the creation of original music. Cage used any recordings in some of his works, as well as frequency test recordings, and Marclay has used second hand records that are sometimes broken up before being stuck back together to form a single disc. Reggae musicians in 1950s and 1960s Jamaica and American club DJs of the 1960s and 1970s also adopted this recycling aspect of postmodernism in the development of manipulation techniques that allowed them to re-work existing records, such as cutting, pasting and rewinding. UK hip-hop turntable teams can neither be solely aligned to modernism, as suggested by Poschardt (1998, pp. 393–7), or postmodernism, as suggested by Brewster and Broughton (1999, pp. 18–20), but instead integrate characteristics of both, continuing the modernist preoccupation with progress, innovation and experimentation whilst integrating the contemporary concerns of postmodernism such as the appropriation and recycling of existing musical texts. The dual existence of both modernist and postmodernist characteristics within one genre is supported by Brooker who regards modernism and postmodernism as 'intimately connected', rather than being in opposition (1999, p. xi). He does not negate the existence of modernism and postmodernism as separate and distinct, but describes there being a continuous movement between them:

> ... between them there is the dialogic traffic of collage and argument, the building and unbuilding of orthodoxies. There is no absolute singular cultural entity or absolute historical break, therefore, and no absolute inside or outside part from the ideological constructions requiring them. (1999, p. 4)

Hip-Hop Turntablism and Progress

Notions of progress are central to the development of team routines. Although the turntablist musicians use existent music to create their routines, the resulting compositions are not based upon previous styles but instead use these to construct something new. When interviewed, Beni G of The Mixologists was asked to place the importance of progression in his work on a scale from one to five, one being not at all important and five being very important. He chose five and reflected on this, referring to the creation of the 2001 team championship routine:

> ... all of these different sounds we were using, a lot of people had never used or heard before. Or they might have heard before, but they hadn't ever thought of using it in a battle routine ... and it wasn't the same old samples being chopped up ... it was refreshing which is what we like to do. It's the same with Tony and Joel [two members of the Scratch Perverts] – they like to do stuff which is fresh and as far as we're concerned that's why we like to do it. We know that here's something that's fresh and new ... then that's really the start of what it's all about – to define your sound ... (Beni G, 2002)

Innovation and Experimentation

Innovation is central to the aims of turntablist musicians to the point where the copying of routines is strictly frowned upon. The turntablists' experimentation with sound and the relationship between the very nature of the genre and its technology have resulted in the development of new and innovative compositional processes, such as the way in which the team has developed a method of working together to create an original composition from existent recordings. Beni G regards the experimentation and the development of new techniques as vitally important in the development of routines:

For me, it can't be stagnant. You've got to push, always be pushing boundaries and Tony and Joel and Neil [members of the Scratch Perverts] are the people that are really doing that, really innovating more than anything – that's their prime focus which is wicked 'cos they're taking it to the next level, pushing it further and further. (Beni G, 2002)

The work of hip-hop turntable teams in the UK also reflects a number of *postmodern* preoccupations, most notably in the blurring of production and consumption and confusions over time and space through the appropriation and re-use of existing texts.

A Blurring of Production and Consumption

Hip-hop turntablism is an act of both production and consumption. Brewster and Broughton (1999), reflecting how it is a characteristic of DJing in general, suggest:

A DJ is a consumer of recorded music: he buys a record and listens to it, just like anyone else might. However, because his audience is listener to it, he is also, *at the exact same time*, making a product – the performance of the music contained in that record. And the choices he makes as a *consumer* (which records he chooses to buy and listen to) are a defining part of his worth as a *producer* (how creative and distinctive he is). (p. 19)

As Paul Willis comments, the musical practices of youth culture suggest that the former distinctions of production and consumption are now less clear-cut and the boundaries are broken down: 'Consumption is itself a kind of self-creation – of identities, or space, of cultural forms – with its own kind of cultural empowerment' (1990, p. 26). Consumption, he reflects, is essentially creative. This blurring of consumption and production is increased in the work of hip-hop turntablists. Team members use records and turntables, previously technologies through which to consume music, to produce original music. They are producers not only because they perform the music contained in records, but also because they continually select and manipulate small samples taken from a number of records which are then combined to create an original routine.

The Appropriation and Re-use of Existing Texts

Hip-hop team turntablism creates original music by assembling samples of existing records from a range of different times and places. Rejecting the linear nature of historical progress, music of the past is used and valued as music of the present and the audience understands the citation of many kinds of music. Although hip-hop team turntable compositions recycle sounds from different times and places, they are held together by a strong artistic intent and structure. In 'Popular Music and Postmodern Theory', Andrew Goodwin warns against a superficial understanding of pastiche that would undervalue the complex and deliberate interplay of music samples found in turntablism:

> ... these critical strategies miss both the historicizing function of sampling technologies in contemporary pop and the ways in which textual incorporation cannot be understood as a 'blank parody'. We need categories to add to pastiche, which demonstrate how contemporary pop opposes, celebrates and promotes the texts it steals from. (1995, p. 81)

The music of UK hip-hop turntable teams reflects the more contemporary preoccupations with postmodernism whilst retaining the characteristics of modernism as championed by earlier turntable musicians such as Maholy-Nagy and Schaeffer. The features of these two cultural trends do not exhibit themselves in tidy, discrete categories. Instead, they are evident in an interweaving of characteristics that are often simultaneously active throughout the creative process, influencing the work at different points and taking shape in relation to each other. Notions of progress are central to the compositional processes of hip-hop turntable teams. Innovation and experimentation are evident not only in formal aspects such as the creation and use of new sound manipulation techniques relating to rhythm, structure and melody but also in the development of collaborative devising processes through which the routines are created. The routines are held together by a strong artistic intent established at the beginning of the devising process that is reflected in the value judgements made throughout. To achieve these modernist ideals however, the hip-hop turntable teams use tools associated with postmodernism. The original routines are constructed from small parts of records containing music from a wide historical and geographical area. Routines are created through both consumption and production of these records, resulting in a recycling of existing material to create new music. Style is important in the presentation of this new music, in both team image and performance practices. In the use of such postmodern means to channel a more modernist spirit, hip-hop turntablism can therefore be regarded as a manifestation of both postmodernism and modernism. The compositional processes of hip-hop turntable teams do not conform solely to either modernism or postmodernism, but instead demonstrate a modernist spirit delivered through postmodern means.

Chapter 4

Turntablism and Technology

The role of technology is central to the discussion of the compositional processes of hip-hop turntablist teams. DJ culture is closely linked with its technical means of production and is simultaneously the cause and result of much of its musical and technological advancement since the 1970s. Poschardt regards the link between DJs and their technology as inseparable, as they were one of the first generations to have grown up in the technological world of TVs, videos, computers and stereo systems. Technology for them is an integral part of life that offers virtually unlimited creative opportunities (1998, p. 365).

The Uses/Abuses of Technology

The DJs' use of the gramophone as a creative rather than solely reproductive instrument sees the musicians extending their use from the inventors' original conception. Poschardt regards DJ culture as being the first artistic avant-garde within popular music that 'recodes modern technology' (1998, p. 358). Usually musically untrained and unfamiliar with the technology-conquering manifestos of the twentieth century artistic avant-garde, the artists of DJ culture follow no rules except, 'if it sounds good, then that [is] enough' (Kempster, 1996, p. 155). Adapting technology to meet their own creative and technological needs became a characteristic of the 'technologically innovative' hip-hop genre, resulting from a desire to experiment, to develop new compositional processes and to create a 'new type of sound experience' (ibid., p. 155).

The creative use of technology, regarded by some as the violation of technology, began at the outset of DJ culture. Poschardt relates this to the inquiring nature of the artists who questioned the creative potential of the record player as practitioners rather than as theorists (Poschardt, 1998, p. 257). Through their actions, turntable musicians developed not only new sounds but also whole new musical genres. Poschardt regards the extension of the turntable's musical purpose as a revolutionary aspect of hip-hop, pointing out that the majority of equipment used by hip hop artists was primarily reproductive and became instruments only through their creative application. Tony Vegas of the hip-hop team The Scratch Perverts comments:

> I understand the stereotype people have of turntables – that it's simply something to play other people's music on ... But this is really becoming an instrument in the way people use it now. It's being taken to a whole other level. (Pemberton, 1998, p. 4)

One aspect of this creative use of technology was the re-configuration of existing technologies to meet the creative, technical and sometimes financial needs of DJs. As Griffiths (1979) comments, electronic music is dependent on the means available at the time of composition and an understanding of electronic music must take into account the creativity displayed by the composers' use of technology available to them. Grandmaster Flash, a qualified electrician, constructed his own version of equipment already on the market to suit his own needs. When trying out DJ Pete Jones' sound-system to see how he cut between tracks so smoothly, Flash realised that the mixer allowed him to hear what the second turntable was playing before it was played out, giving the DJ greater control. Flash recognised that this function was enabled by a particular switch, and installed one in his own system so that he too could anticipate records. Poschardt regards such an appropriation and adaptation of existing technologies as being one of the first instances of the artist/inventor, in contrast to the separate roles of designer/engineer and composer/performer that had existed previously. Some of the new sounds resulting from the creative use of existing technologies however, were created quite simply by accident. The technique of scratching for example, central to the music of hip-hop turntablists, is reputed to have been discovered accidentally by DJ Theodore when his mother interrupted his mixing practice. What was at first regarded by the music technology industries as a violation of their equipment became seen as a creative act borne out of a growing demand for instruments that met the needs of DJs. This in turn, prompted the industry to develop instruments that met the requirements of turntable musicians.

The Equipment of the Contemporary Hip-Hop Turntablist

The difficulty of discussing the musical equipment used by hip-hop turntable teams is that, as Griffiths remarks, electronic music is a new art still in a state of rapid development. Each month yet more equipment is manufactured, and while it may not make the existing equipment redundant, it will offer artists new creative opportunities. Although manufacturers are always improving and re-designing the equipment, that used by the hip-hop turntable teams remains fundamentally the same – turntables and mixers. To overcome the difficulty of discussing such rapidly-developing music technology, I shall discuss the majority of equipment through instrument type rather than specific models. I shall however, refer specifically to the Technics turntables, as they have remained the definitive hip-hop turntable for the past 20 years.

The Turntables

The first turntables used by DJs tended to be borrowed from the family home or were machines generally found in the domestic environment and converted for the purpose. Often, the musicians could not afford more than one turntable and so music on tape was mixed with one record at a time. Since then, developments in turntable technology have been in reaction to the creative and technical working needs of DJs and, in turn, have influenced their creative output. Pemberton states that the development of the technical skills of the DJs coupled with improvements in turntable technology has led to the dramatic evolution of the art form. DJ Pogo, UK DMC mixing champion adds:

> Only now are we starting to get proper technical equipment to make our jobs better ... I don't think it necessarily makes your job any easier – it just raises the stakes of what you can do. It broadens your mind to try different things. (Pemberton, 1998, p. 4)

In 1980, Technics manufactured the Technics 1100, the first turntable to meet the creative and technical needs of the DJ. In 1984 these were followed by the Technics 1200 MK2 turntable, '... a magic weapon that allowed DJs to do whatever they wanted', that would become DJ culture's instrument of reference (Poschardt, 1998, p. 235). In their application as an instrument rather than merely a reproductive device, the Technics turntables would change the shape of music history (ibid., p. 235). The Technics 1200s offered DJs many features to make elements of their art easier, or even possible. Although some of these features were relatively simple they were of huge importance, for example the easily located big start and stop button on the top of the turntable and the variable height record light, both of which were vital when working in the dark environments of night clubs. The Technics 1200s boast a direct drive motor that has the advantage of a minimal start-up and breaking time and the turntable speed is controlled via a high-precision pitch control, operated by a thumb-wide pitch regulator. The pitch regulation allows speed variations as little as 0.01 per cent thus allowing the precise mixing of records even over long periods. The tone arm is height-adjustable and is held in friction free gimbal suspension and the stylus weight can be adjusted from 0 to 2.5 grams, which allows DJs to adapt the 1200s to their own specification. Poschardt states that part of the reason for the 1200s' popularity is that they are considered indestructible. Protected against vibration from speakers or monitors by a floor of cast aluminium, the turntables also have an aluminium head shell constructed from a single piece of metal and an anti-vibration rubber fitted to both sides of the turntable. These factors, coupled with the robustness of the direct drive motor, ensure that the turntables keep working throughout even the longest performances.

The Mixer

Poschardt describes the DJ's mixer as '… the true instrument of synthesis' (1998, p. 237). Alongside the developments of the turntable, the mixer was one of the first pieces of musical equipment specifically designed to meet the needs of the DJ. The mixer connects the turntables and allows the records playing on them to be mixed together. Although similar in design to the larger studio mixing desks, the modern DJ mixer is a small box, usually smaller than the turntables that it sits between. The contemporary mixer boasts a number of functions that allow the DJ to choose and mix sounds and passages from the chosen sound sources to create a new composition – the level faders, cross fader, line switch and equalizer. The level faders control the volume of the sound sources connected to individual channels. The cross fader connects the two turntable channels. If the fader is pushed to the left, the turntable connected to the left channel is heard, if the fader is pushed to the right the turntable connected to the right channel is heard and if placed in the middle, both turntables are heard simultaneously. The line switch allows individual channels to be switched off instantly. A highly skilled user of the switch would be able to mix only the bass drum of one track into another track whilst the rest of the track would remain inaudible. Precise use of this switch is vital to genres such as hip-hop as the backspin should not be heard when executing specific scratch techniques. The equalizer allows the DJ to separate the sounds that fall into the high, middle and low frequencies of a record. Records can be deconstructed into their frequency layers and then reconstructed using elements from the original tracks. As Poschardt describes, the DJ could remove all frequencies except scraps of melody or percussion patterns. In a similar way to the development of much musical equipment utilised by DJ culture, the mixing desk has developed in relation to the needs expressed by DJs. Philip Farrer suggests that this requirement comes partly from the audience on the dancefloor who have become more discerning about the performance and demand increased levels of control and sound quality (1998, p. 46).

The Choice of Turntables

The choice and use of turntables differs between those composers who chose to use the newest technology available and those who chose to work with older, technologically surpassed models. Moholy-Nagy, working with turntables in the 1920s and 1930s, was faced with working with extremely crude hardware, the gramophone only recently beginning to benefit from technical improvements such as electrical powering and the refinement of membranes. Similarly, Schaeffer's turntable compositions of the 1940s and 1950s were created using basic recording equipment – a basic 78 rpm disk-cutting lathe and four turntables that limited the range and use of manipulation techniques. The recording medium suffered from poor audio quality that affected the timbre (Manning, 2003, pp. 6–7) and in using the then-standard size ten-inch records, the recording time was restricted to little more than three minutes. The use of 78 rpm also affected the looping techniques as the duration of each loop lasted for only 0.8 seconds. Lowering the speed of rotation could lengthen the loop length, but any adjustment further than 30 rpm (which only increased the loop's duration to 2 seconds) would result is a substantial degeneration in sound quality (ibid., p. 7). Manning describes how this limited technology directly affected Schaeffer's creative output:

> Even the construction of a simple montage, joining a number of different segments together to create a freshly recorded sequence of sound events, demanded an elaborate set of studio procedures to line up and accurately cue the constituent recordings on different turntables. (ibid., p. 7)

Whilst these examples may seem basic in comparison to the turntables and recording equipment available to the contemporary composer, they were at the time the newest technology available. Hindemith, Toch, Moholy-Nagy and Schaeffer were in the fortunate position of working for larger artistic research and development bodies; Hindemith and Toch working at the Hochschule für Musik in Berlin, Moholy-Nagy working as part of the Bauhaus in Dessau and Schaeffer as part of Radiodiffusion Française, which supported their turntable-based experiments both financially and artistically. Schaeffer was also involved in the development of new turntable technologies himself and through his investigations into how best to perform his compositions live, designed and built one of the earliest sound systems, incorporating multiple turntables, mixers and loudspeaker units (Chadabe, 1997). Moholy-Nagy and Schaeffer were not primarily interested in the turntable's potential as a musical instrument but used it because it was the most suitable equipment for their explorations into the nature of sound. For this reason both composers abandoned the turntable as soon as new technologies for the recording and playback of sound were developed, Moholy-Nagy turning to the possibilities of manipulating optical soundtracks as used with moving film, and Schaeffer turning to tape-based composition in his purpose-built studio provided by Radiodiffusion Française.

In contrast to Moholy-Nagy and Schaeffer, turntable composer Christian Marclay used equipment that in relation to contemporary turntable technology was old and technologically surpassed, even using turntables that he found in junk shops and car boot sales. Using old Califone turntables, Marclay embraced the quirks of his vintage equipment and the creative potential of the older technology. For him, mistakes driven by the technology, for example a record making a sound that was not the intention of the original recording artist, are an exciting occurrence demonstrating the creative potential of turntable music.

Club DJs did not share Marclay's passion for technical obsolescence, but in their creative use of the turntable utilised the most advanced equipment available to them. For almost all of the early club DJs this led to the construction of homemade or basic systems that would enable them to undertake the record manipulations that they wished to develop. In the 1960s, DJ Terry Noel worked with the sound engineer at the nightclub *Arthur*, to create independently operated speakers with separate frequency controls enabling him to move sounds around the venue (ibid., p. 63). Fellow DJ Francis Grasso benefited from the first ever stereo mixer that allowed the cueing of records, built by engineer Alex Rosner:

> The cueing system was one of my old fashioned adventures ... It was really primitive and not very good. But it did the job. And nobody could complain because there was nothing else around. (ibid., p. 135)

The Choice of Records

The use of records is central to the composition of turntable music and each composer chooses and uses records to reflect his or her compositional objectives. Schaeffer used records that were created specifically for use in their composition and made his own recordings with a disc-cutting lathe. He created discs that contained various captured sounds, for example sounds from toy shops and percussion instruments used in *Etude aux Tourniquets* (1948) and sounds from saucepans and canal boats in his composition *Etude Pathetique* (1948). Disc recordings of more traditional instrumental sounds of piano and orchestra were made and used in compositions including *Etude pour Piano and Orchestra* and *Etude Violette* (1948). The turntable compositions of Cage and Marclay use existing records that were not produced specifically for this creative use. Cage's *Imaginary Landscape No. 3* (1943) calls for the performer to use frequency test recordings and *Imaginary Landscape No. 5* (1952) asks the performer to use sound material from forty-two phonograph records from any source, reassembled in fragments structured according to chance. Cage's installation *33 1/3* (1969) asked visitors to select any record from a stand and to play them on multiple turntables. Marclay uses records bought from junk shops and charity shops, using them as 'musical instruments' (artshole.co.uk). By incorporating the old, used nature of these recordings in his compositions he celebrates the sounds and effects that result from the deterioration of the record.

For club DJs the manipulation techniques they developed did not rely on their choice of records. Records were chosen to create a nightclub experience, which was always foremost in the mind of the DJ, and any manipulation techniques that were used were to heighten and enhance this experience for the dance floor.

Reasons for Turntable Experimentation

The different uses of the turntables and records as well as the music composed with them clearly reflected the composers' artistic objectives. The composers discussed in this chapter can be placed into two categories of artistic aims – those for whom turntable experimentation was used in the exploration and development of new musical languages and those composers who used turntables to create and communicate an artistic concept.

The Exploration and Development of New Musical Languages

One of the first uses of turntables to develop a new musical language was undertaken by Moholy-Nagy, scratching into gramophone records:

> Grooves are incised by human agency into the wax plate, without any external mechanical means, which then produce sound effects that would signify – without new instruments and without an orchestra – a fundamental innovation in sound production (of new, hitherto unknown sounds and tonal relations) both in composition and in musical performance. (Moholy-Nagy, 1922, cited in Katz, 1992, p. 105)

This work explored the possibilities of producing a new 'graphic mechanical scale' (Moholy-Nagy, 1989 [1922], p. 56) where, as Katz describes, '... a wax-inscribed character would not only represent a specific sound, it would *cause* that sound if "read" by a phonograph needle' (pp. 105–6). Ernst Toch felt that his phonograph experimentations attempted to extend the phonograph's function, to create 'a characteristic music of its own' (Toch (1930), cited in Katz (2005), p. 102).

Transforming the turntable from a reproductive to productive instrument raised questions regarding the sound world available to composers, pioneering the creative use of turntable technology and the new sounds made available. Schaeffer, in his experimental use of turntables, searched for new ways to record, playback and combine everyday sounds to create a music that was constructed from natural sounds rather than from traditional instruments:

> This determination to compose with materials taken from an existing collection of experimental sounds, I name "Musique Concrete" to mark well the place in which we find ourselves, no longer dependent upon preconceived sounds abstractions, but now using fragments of sound existing concretely and considered as sound objects defined and whole ... (Chadabe, 1997, pp. 26–7)

Cage, like Moholy-Nagy, was interested in the record's creative potential and his experiments with turntables were a continuation of his exploration into the use of noise as sound source for music. His prophetic comments, made during a speech to the Seattle Arts Society in 1937, looked to a time when music would be produced by electronic instruments that would enable all sounds to be used for musical purposes. Like Moholy-Nagy and Schaeffer, Cage looked to create a new musical language that would offer the composer the entire field of sound and time. For Cage, the turntables offer unparalleled potential to deliver this new music:

> We want to capture and control these sounds, to use them not as studio effects but as musical instruments. Every film studio has a library of "sound effects" recorded on film. With a film phonograph it is now possible to control the amplitude and frequency of any one of these sounds and to give to it rhythms within or beyond the reach of the imagination. Given four film phonographs, we can compose and perform a quartet for explosive motor, wind, heartbeat and landslide. (Cage, 1937)

For Moholy-Nagy, Schaeffer and Cage, the main focus of turntable experimentation was on questioning and developing the nature of sound itself, and of how to use these sounds, integrating them into a coherent and structured composition.

The Development and Reflection of an Artistic Concept

For Marclay, the main area of focus is the development and reflection of an artistic concept. Although he creates compositions that question the nature of sound and music, his major artistic focus is not the development of a new musical language. Marclay's turntable compositions partly deal with issues of history, exploring the concept of vinyl as a 'living capsule of sound', constantly changing through age (Newman, 2002). Through his interest in recycling and the making of new music from discarded records, Marclay is able to acknowledge the past whilst simultaneously rejecting it (Gross, 1998). An important aspect of Marclay's composition work is the concept of recording and its relationship with the listener. Marclay regards recording as becoming the main medium through which people listen to music and their reference point for an understanding and enjoyment of the music. In an interview with Gross, Marclay comments that his work aims to underline the awareness of recorded music and its impact on the listener by bringing the residual sounds of the records (for example the hisses, pops and scratches) to the fore of his compositions, highlighting the medium of vinyl as a 'cheap slab of plastic' (ibid.). In the live performances of his compositions, Marclay aims to increase the level of intensity he regards as missing in the original recorded music through raising the audience's awareness of the manipulation processes, the visual actions informing the listening (ibid.).

The developments of turntable-based sound manipulation techniques within popular music grew organically from the artists' work as club DJs. For them, the turntable was not a new instrument to be incorporated into their artistic practice but was rather the tool of their trade. Through their musical investigations they developed new approaches to their work, regarding the playing of records as '... a creative, musical process' (Poschardt, 1998, p. 107). However, the same environment that led these DJs to develop turntable-based sound manipulation techniques also limited them in other live creative developments. As club DJs, their musical impetus came from a desire to create and sustain a successful nightclub experience through the relationship between themselves, the records and the dance floor, rather than to achieve any artistic goal. Francis Grasso never saw himself as an artist, but merely as someone who played and mixed records to satisfy himself and his crowd (Poschardt, 1998, p. 108). Even the studio-based remix compositions of Walter Gibbons and Frankie Knuckles that developed from the popularity of turntable-based extended tracks were created from a desire to make music that worked more successfully in the club environment, rather than the development of music itself.

Recent Technological Developments

Digital technologies are not new to DJing. CD decks have been on the market for a number of years, and whilst have been accepted into club DJing have not made such an impact on hip hop turntablism. White (1996) contests:

> It is simply not as easy to manipulate a compact disc as it is to work with a vinyl disc and needle. The precision, control and nuance which the turntablist brings to the turntables, especially in live situations, cannot be duplicated with a CD without a great sacrifice of creativity and individuality ...

Digital Vinyl Systems

More recently, manufacturers have been developing both hardware and software-based DJ technologies that enable the hands-on manipulation of digital audio. DVSs (Digital Vinyl Systems) are hardware and software-based systems that allow music on a computer to be controlled by vinyl, CD, MIDI or supported USB controllers. By doing so, they integrate the traditional analogue DJ set-up of turntables and a mixer with digital audio files stored and accessed via a computer. These systems enable turntablists to perform with digital audio by controlling the software parameters using their traditional hardware. Therefore, turntable musicians are able to use established techniques, but with digital audio files. As well as allowing the continuation of established techniques, DVS systems also include additional tools including those for looping, cueing, live remixing, re-editing, effects, tempo awareness and key-locking, and offer visual feedback as well as the ability to sync up with supported external hardware.

As Ed Montano remarks, DVS systems keep vinyl central to DJing (2010, p. 399), allowing turntablists to retain techniques and skills that they would have used on more traditional systems. In the article 'Is Digital DJing Killing The Art?' (2011), DJ Maurice Norris reflects:

> ... the act itself of moving something backwards and forwards while combining it with rapid, rhythmically precise on/off movements of a fader (or button) is much less likely to die because of the unique sound it makes and the skill required to do this effectively will remain the same for many years to come. The sound of an "Ahhh" or "Freshhh" scratch and the manipulation of them is so ingrained now in hip hop culture that these will always be the staple sounds of a turntablist and ones that, for the time being at least, require a high level of skill to manipulate well.

Whilst DVS systems support established techniques, the possibilities presented by using digital audio, manipulated live using a variety of different controllers alongside turntables, may also lead to new ones.

Implications for Hip-Hop Turntablism

In November 2010, Panasonic announced that it had ceased production of its analogue Technics turntables, reflecting what the manufacturers described as 'the accelerating transformation of the entire audio market from analogue to digital' (www.residentadvisor.net). This situation was compounded by a dwindling of component suppliers, which made sourcing parts difficult and costly. In October 2010, the DMC had announced that the former DMC World DJ Championships sponsors, Technics, would be replaced by Serato and Rane, manufacturers of digital DJing products. From 2011, both the World DJ Championship and DJ Team Championship would permit the use of a Digital DJ System (Serato Scratch Live) alongside traditional vinyl, 'in order to balance traditional mixing and the popularity of digital vinyl playback' (Settle, 2010). In the DMC World DJ Championship 2011 (solo event), competitors were permitted to use up to two Technics turntables, an analogue or digital mixer and any brand DVS. Whilst there were no restrictions on the DVS settings, no other devices were permitted. Similarly, for the DMC World DJ Team Championship, teams were permitted to use Technics turntables with analogue and digital mixers as well as any DVS, but in addition competitors were also able to use loop stations, external hardware and MPCs. The DMC Battle for World Supremacy rules however, still restricted the competitors to two Technics turntables and a mixer without effects (www.dmcdjchamps.com, 2011).

How are hip-hop turntablists using this new technology? A-Track (2008), former DMC World Champion, discussed his experience of DJing with Serato Scratch Live:

> Any scratch that I can do on a normal record, I can do it on Scratch Live because it's a normal record ... really it's the same feel and the response is really accurate, so it's good. It allows me to have a big collection of records without carrying around like 32 boxes ... just to carry that many records, it's just not really possible.

DJ Rocc (2011) from the turntablist crew The Beat Junkies reflects on the effect that DVS has had on DJing so far:

> The thing about Serato is, it's changed the way that everyone DJs. It made people that enjoy music want to be a DJ but it made the DJs who are really DJs like superman almost.

DJ Shiftee (2011) describes the creation of a routine by himself and DJs Rafik and Qbert, explaining how the team used the DVS. The record described by DJ Shiftee is a time-coded Traktor Scratch Control Vinyl, with a time-coded signal on one side and scratch samples on the other:

> ... we had division of parts. We started all on the Traktor side of the vinyl, so using all tracks in Traktor ... Qbert was the drummer ... he was working with the original song and just working with the kick and snare next to each other ... We went into the half-time breakdown where I triggered "it's time" and the notes of the melody ... so I do something a little bit tricky and I take my finger and brush it against the side of the turntable to create a variation in pitch ... So sort of our structure was attack the song, recreate it, do a little breakdown but after the breakdown I'd let the track play on deck A ... now while we were doing that breakdown, Rafik was flipping the record to the other side and preparing his "ah" sound, so as soon as I dropped the beat ... Rafik was right there on the one cutting the "ah" ... While Rafik was scratching, Qbert ... flipped the record over to go to the vinyl side and cut it up fresh ...

The process DJ Shiftee describes is no different to the process when using a traditional turntablist set-up, but involves using new technologies integrated into the system, for example controllers. The turntables are used in the same way as in traditional set-ups, and indeed DVS systems are promoted by manufacturers in terms of how similar it feels to the traditional manipulation methods:

> Traktor Scratch offers a 2khz control signal, embedded onto high quality, 120g vinyl, which makes ultra fast scratching, backspins and even motor-offs feel as if your tracks were cut directly onto 12". (nativeinstruments.com)

On the Native Instruments Youtube Channel, former DMC World Champion DJ Craze showcases the Traktor Scratch Pro and Traktor Scratch Pro 2 DVS. Again, the description of how he uses the system relates directly to traditional turntablist techniques:

> ... Craze simultaneously triggers cue points on both decks, while still staying true to his roots with some serious beatjuggling. By combining traditional vinyl techniques like juggling, scratching and body tricks with advanced controller-based functions such as cue point manipulation, tempo-synced effects and ultra-quick track changes, this performance showcases the cutting edge of turntablism and controllerism using the latest digital DJing technology. (Native Instruments, 2010)

and

> A beat juggling section in the middle leads to the finale where Craze combines fast cue-point juggles and vocal samples with the integrated Traktor effects. All things combined, this latest Turntable Tricknology routine effectively highlights the vastly expanded creative potential of the new Traktor generation. (Native Instruments, 2011)

How the New Technologies May Affect the Creative Practice of Turntablism

The use of digital audio, rather than reliance on vinyl, opens up a world of possibilities for hip-hop turntablists, A-Trak (2008) commenting, 'I can scratch on something that's not even on vinyl yet ...'. As discussed earlier in this Chapter, hip-hop turntablism has close relationships with the technology on which it is made. As the article 'Is Digital DJing Killing the Art?' DJ Maurice Norris reflects;

> ... isn't this what hip hop is all about anyway? ... Hip-hop is about taking what you've got (usually very little) and doing something new with it. And this is exactly what the early pioneers like DJ Kool Herc and the newer turntablists/ controllerists were and are doing with their experimental use equipment ... they're not just relying on the tool itself. In fact, it's more the case that the need for the tool was born out of the ideas they had in the first place ... Much like the hip hop pioneers of old, good DJs will bend the rules of this newly available technology and make it their own, injecting their personality into what was once a "static" piece of kit or one that was intended for another purpose. (2011)

The manufacturers of Digital Vinyl Systems such as Serato and Native Instruments recognize the importance of experimentation in turntablism and have placed innovation at the centre of their marketing. Native Instruments' description of their

Traktor Scratch systems for example, states '... it's easy to try new techniques and develop new skills ...' (www.nativeinstruments.com). This aspect of the innovative creative opportunities presented by DVS is also reflected in comments from the DMC. As part of the official statement from DMC on the announcement that Serato would now be sponsoring the championships, Sally Mclintock (DMC's World Championship Manager) reflected how through the manufacturer's support, 'the creative landscape has now been widened' (Settle, 2010). Tony Prince (DMC Founder) commented on the way in which DVS systems will positively influence hip-hop turntablism:

> I know the DJs will take up this new creative challenge and bring their art to a
> new level no one can presently imagine ... Expanding the DJ's creative potential
> is what the DMC has always encouraged ... I just can't wait to see where the DJs
> will take us with Serato supporting their musical creativity and inspiration in the
> years ahead ... we're about to produce the next generation of DJs, the DJs of a
> new breed ... my message to the next generation is to unharness their creative
> ability [and] check out the new possibilities ... (Settle, 2010)

Dean Standing from Rane Corporation, who also sponsor the DMC World Championships, suggests that using DVS systems will enable DJs to 'further push the limits of their craft' (Settle, 2010).

DVS tools exist to replace vinyl with digital audio as the main sound source for DJs, and aim to emulate the use of analogue technology (vinyl) through digital means, Lippit (2006) remarking how 'Simulation and efficiency of existing practice' is the primary focus of these DVS. Whilst the manufacturers stress the creative potential of these systems, Lippit feels that such digital tools 'do not necessarily open the doors to new musical expression ... artistic experimentation is difficult or just not possible. These products promote a future that only evokes the familiar past' (2006, p. 71). The importance of vinyl to turntablism to date cannot be ignored. Michael Endelman (2002) remarks:

> Hip-hop DJs are a stubborn and purist bunch, dedicated to the pairing of vinyl
> and turntables for reasons romantic as well as rational. In a genre that is obsessed
> with notions of authenticity, vinyl signifies a connection to hip-hop's historical
> lineage, which starts with those South Bronx pioneers who began a global
> movement with little more than two turntables and a microphone.

The article 'Digitizing the DJ' suggests that the importance of vinyl records is disappearing from the genre and that the technology used impacts on the performance processes and creative energies of the hip hop DJ Mark Katz (2005) discusses the effects of digital technology on hip-hop turntablism, remarking how 'many feel that the art is diminished when the craft is made easier. Others lament the loss of a strong sense of authenticity surrounding turntables and pre-recorded discs' (p. 121). In the article 'Is Digital DJing Killing The Art?', DJ Maurice

Norris questions whether the new technology is making DJs lazy and whether the use of tools such as the sync button is cheating:

> Debate has raged since the appearance of CDJs in the late '90s as to whether using shortcuts like cue points and auto beatmatching is considered cheating or not. There's also the concern that the more traditional analog style of scratching and beat juggling will die out giving rise to what's been labelled as "controllerism" and digital manipulation. (2011)

For some, the use of DVS has been a positive force for hip-hop turntablism, hip-hop pioneer DJ Jazzy Jeff commenting that Serato Scratch Live '… saved two turntables and a mixer' (2006). In *Popular Music: The Key Concepts*, Roy Shuker (2002) reflects how new recording technologies offer new creative possibilities, and can provide the foundation for new genres (p. 281). But can the tools offered by DVS, such as looping, cueing and tempo awareness, really be seen as offering creative opportunities for turntablism? In the words of DJ Maurice Norris (2011), 'The tool itself doesn't make you the DJ, it's your own style, your ideas and creative use of whatever you have got to hand that does'. The use of DVS systems redefines the art and craft of the DJ (ibid., p. 398), generating new understandings and interpretations of DJ practice (Montano, 2010, p. 404):

> As DJ Culture expands its techniques, it expands its language. As it develops its language, DJs are able to broaden their expression. As DJs further the potential to express themselves, they evolve the DJ-as-artist paradigm. (Emsley, 2011, p. 14)

Chapter 5
The Creation of Original Sound Material

In the creation of original compositions from records, members of hip-hop turntable teams use a variety of sound manipulation techniques. The basic techniques used by the teams were established by the late 1970s (Poschardt, 1998, p. 173) and over the following four decades have been developed and added to, both reflecting and responding to the growing artistic needs of the turntablists. Although there are many parallels between the sound manipulation techniques of the hip-hop turntable teams and those of their predecessors and contemporaries in the world of experimental art music, by and large the musicians were unaware of such concurrent activities (Kahn, 2003, p. 17). This Chapter will establish the main manipulation techniques used by the hip-hop turntable teams and discuss the implications of these in the development of new musical processes. It does not aim to give detailed instructions about how the various techniques are executed, as this information is already easily available in a wide range of instructional DJ books such as Brewster and Broughton's *How to DJ (Properly)* (2002) and videos including *A Vestax Master-Class* (1998) and *So you Wanna be a DJ* (1996). To look at these techniques in more detail I have divided them into three categories – structural techniques, including the breakbeat, general mixing, punchphasing and backspinning; rhythmic techniques, including scratching and beat-juggling; and melodic techniques, including the creation of melodies via the turntables' bass, tone and pitch controls.

Structural Compositional Techniques

The Breakbeat

In the early 1970s the breakbeat was invented by a young Bronx DJ, DJ Kool Herc and, according to Poschardt, laid the roots of hip-hop music. When working in the discos, Herc noticed that there were certain sections of a record – usually the drum break – that the dancers would respond more to. In response to this, he began to extend the excitement generated during these sections by playing breaks one after another, omitting the rest of the track. DJ Afrika Bambaata describes how Herc then began to play with two copies of the same record, extending the break even further using two turntables:

> He took the music of like Mandrill, like "Fencewalk", certain disco records that had funky percussion breaks like The Incredible Bongo Band when they came

out with "Apache", and he just kept that beat *going*. It might be that certain part of the record that everybody waits for – they just let their inner self go and get wild. (David Toop, in Forman and Neal (eds), pp. 235–6)

Through this early development of DJ compositional techniques, Herc had extended the DJ's position from the archivist of records to a musician and an author.

Mixing

The mixing technique instigated by DJ Kool Herc through the linking of his breakbeats was very basic – tracks were faded into one another with no attempt to cut one track into the other or even to keep a steady beat going. Another young DJ, Grandmaster Flash, was inspired enough by the compositional implications of the breakbeat and frustrated enough by Herc's lack of mixing talent that by 1974, following a long period of experimentation into the creative possibilities of the turntable, he had developed a number of working practices which enabled a more aesthetically satisfying mixing technique via turntables:

> I called my style "Quick Mix Theory", which is taking a section of music and cutting it on time, back to back, in thirty seconds or less. I was basically to take a particular passage of music and re-arrange the arrangement by way of rubbing the record back and forth or cutting the record, or backspinning the record. (Grandmaster Flash, cited in Brewster and Broughton, 1999, p. 200)

Flash also developed his 'Clock Theory' (ibid., p. 200), which, through markings on the record label, enabled him to almost instantly identify the required section of the record to be played. Through these techniques Flash had developed a method to restructure musical text at will, supported by the adaptation of his own sound system to incorporate a pre-hear capacity into the mixer so that each turntable could be heard solely by the DJ before it was played out.

Punchphasing and Backspinning

Flash developed two further mixing techniques that also became fundamental compositional techniques of hip-hop – punchphasing and backspinning. Punchphasing allows the DJ to incorporate shorter stabs of sound from one record over the breakbeat from another record, enriching and re-interpreting the original musical text. Flash's technique of back-spinning allows the DJ to quickly rewind a part of the music that s/he wants to repeat and can be achieved two ways – the 'Dog Paddle', where the record is spun back from its outer rim, and the 'Phone Dial', where it is spun back from the middle. In both these techniques the reverse motion can either be heard as a squeaky sound effect or is in silence, depending on the position of the mixers' cross fader.

The central compositional processes of mixing frequently bring a range of diverse music together in the creation of an original piece of hip-hop. Charlie Chase, DJ for the Cold Crush Brothers comments:

> This was the only time, this was the only kind of music where you could hear James Brown playing with … Aerosmith! You can just … mix two bands together … [We] were there to listen to all era's music, you could just mix it together … It was weird, but it sounded good. (Ibid., p. 207)

The main concern for the hip-hop DJ is not for the record that has been sampled, but for its effectiveness as sonic components within the new composition. Afrika Bambaataa, named 'master of records' due to his huge knowledge of music and his extensive record archive, was known for his eclectic mix of music that went into his compositions. He demonstrated to other DJs that a wide range of music that could be used in the creation of hip-hop. His 1982 record *Planet Rock* was no exception, incorporating elements from Kraftwerk's *Trans Europe Express* and *Numbers*, the beat from Captain Sky's *Super Sperm*, parts of Babe Ruth's *The Mexican* as well as sections of Malcolm X's speeches. Brewster comments that *Planet Rock* demonstrated the way in which sampled elements can be manipulated rather than preserved intact, and how they can be 'collided into each other and woven into an intricate new sound tapestry' (ibid., p. 227).

Rhythmic Compositional Techniques

Scratching

The technique of scratching can be traced back to the early 1930s in the phonograph experiments of members of the Bauhaus movement, László Moholy-Nagy, Oskar Fischinger and Paul Arma, who attempted to alter the acoustical content of records by running them against the stylus to scratch new patterns. However, it was not until the development of DJ culture that scratching became a source of sound manipulation fundamental to compositional technique. The use of scratching within DJ culture – moving the record back and forth against the stylus with one hand whilst using the cross-fade of the mixing desk – is reputed to have been discovered accidentally by DJ Theodore when his mother interrupted his mixing practice. Hans Keller (1981) describes the techniques of scratching pioneer DJ Theodore:

> On the left, for example, "Heartbeat" is running, and on the right he's just put on a particular record, he accurately puts the needle somewhere near the centre, and, with brief jerks to the rim of the record, he introduces a syncopated, rapid machine gun rhythm. He pushes the switch on the mixing box to the left, says something to his assistant, who reaches into a box to take out another record.

> Same again, only that this time what comes out is a choppy bass run ... the imagination is given free rein. (1981, p. 47)

Since these early hip-hop pioneers, scratching as a compositional technique has developed further to embrace a range of sonic manipulation. DJ Pogo reflects:

> What's happening is that, as opposed to scratching records just to make a "scratchy" noise, people are now looking at the sounds and trying to change them in any way they can. (Pemberton, 1998, p. 4)

Brewster and Broughton describe how through scratching, the DJ chops up the music into individual notes, beats and noises, allowing him/her to play and manipulate sounds. DJ Tony Vegas, member of the Scratch Perverts team, aligns this to the way in which traditional musicians create from notes (Pemberton, 1998, p .6). Through the use of the pitch control and the different applications of pressure to the record by the DJs' hand the sounds can be dramatically altered, 'creating something new using noise, sound and feeling' (ibid., p. 6). DJ Q-Bert of the Invisibl Skratch Piklz crew comments:

> Manipulating sound with just your hand is like a miracle. The basic root of scratching is that the turntable is an instrument: you're figuring out all these time signatures and rhythms and patterns and notes. (Brewster and Broughton, 1999, p. 239)

The techniques of sonic manipulation covered under the term 'scratching' are varied, and in many instances complex. One of the most basic forms is open-fader scratching, merely the backward and forward motion of the hand on the turntable with no use of the mixer. Another basic pattern is cutting, which incorporates one of the simplest methods of using the mixers cross-fader in a scratch technique. Only the forward motion of the sound is heard as the DJ closes the fader as the hand on the turntable moves backwards. During the early to mid eighties these two manipulation techniques were the mainstay of the hip-hop DJs' repertoire. As rhythmic scratching became more complex, the need arose for more complex scratching techniques. In the mid-eighties the landmark transformer scratch was pioneered by Philadelphian DJs including Spinbad, Cash Money and Jazzy Jeff and is cited in the *A Vestax Master-Class* (1998) as being one of the largest leaps in the evolution of scratch techniques. The hand on the turntable simply moves the record back and forth and the majority of the work is done by the hand on the cross-fader or the line switch of the mixer, cutting the noise in and out. DJ Q-Bert from the American turntable team the Invisibl Skratch Piklz explains:

> You're messing with the whole sound from beginning to end. If the word was "*hello*", it would be like "*h-he-he-ell-ell-lo-o-o-o*". If you were cutting, you'd be getting the beginning of the note: "*h-h-he-he-he-hello*". (Peter Shapiro, 1997, p. 21)

Transforming necessitates careful manipulation of the mixer's cross-fade switch and allows a basic scratch to be chopped up in a variety of new ways, not only giving the DJ more control over the sound, but also making the scratch more flexible and percussive.

In the development of the flare scratch, DJ Flare helped to revolutionise contemporary scratching. The rhythm is achieved by using the cross fader to cut sound out rather than cutting sound in, which leads to a much faster technique than transforming without much movement. Related to this single-click flare is the double-click flare, where the DJ cuts the sound out with two movements of the cross-fader. Once more, the hand on the turntable simply moves the record back and forth. The Orbit scratch, pioneered by DJ Disc, is an extension of this technique and is essentially a double-click flare performed at twice the speed of the accompanying beat. To perform the Crab scratch, introduced by Q-Bert in 1996, the DJ's thumb pushes the cross-fader to one side and two, three or four fingers of the same hand push it back momentarily to the other. This takes a fraction of a second and, meanwhile, the other hand manoeuvres the record:

> Instead of grabbing the fader with your thumb and one other finger, you grab it with all your fingers. It's in the realm of transforming. Instead of going, "da-duh-duh-duh-duh-duh-duh" which is the average speed of transforming, or [he rolls a series of "r"s very quickly], which is the speed of flaring, the crab is like [goes crazy with his mouth]. It's really, really fast. (Q-Bert in Shapiro, 1997, p. 21)

Q-Bert denies that new scratches are being developed solely to provide faster techniques:

> You can do a crab really slowly. What it does though is it broadens your range of expression. Without that technique you can't get to the higher realm. You can do much more patterns ... (Shapiro, 1997, p. 21)

Scratch techniques such as those described above are not only performed in isolation, but are often combined to create unique patterns.

Beat Juggling

Beat juggling is the manipulation of two identical records on two separate turntables, quickly alternating between them to create original patterns. The technique was developed as late as 1990 by Barry B (from Doug E Fresh's Get Fresh Crew) and Steve Dee (from the X-Men crew). Brewster and Broughton assert that beat juggling is undoubtedly an act of musical creativity, referring to the hip-hop DJ Roc Raida, 1995 DMC World Champion:

> The result is an impossibly complex pattern of improvised drumming; he seems to be able to put each beat exactly where he wants it ... he then speeds up the

pattern in a ballistic sequence of funky syncopation and double beats. It sounds ... nothing like the original records. (Brewster and Broughton, 1999, p. 244)

The manipulation technique of beat juggling can be divided into three main processes; the loop, where short pattern is repeated; the breakdown, where the DJ halts the record between each beat to slow down the pattern; and the fill, where the beats from the second record are integrated with those of the first, either to double or triple the beats or to produce an echo effect using the cross-fader. Hip-hop DJ Rob Swift explains:

> Let's say a record is playing, with your fingers you tap the record gently on beat, so you're breaking down each noise on the record. You're breaking down the kick, the hi-hat, the snare. It's like everything is slowed down. In 1990 Steve Dee [also a member of the X-Men] is credited with actually taking records and re-arranging them like a sampler; making beats and stuff like that ... He would do patterns and beats with it. (Shapiro, 1997, p. 21)

Melodic Compositional Techniques

Hip-hop turntablists have developed methods to create original melodies through using the controls of the turntables. DJ Pogo, a pioneer in the integration of turntables into established musical traditions, describes how when playing with jazz musician Courtney Pine they were able to chase each others' melodies by the DJ using the bass tone and pitch control to make melodies and bass-lines. In 1983, hip-hop musician D.ST won Best R&B Instrumental Performance for his input on Herbie Hancock's single *Rockit*, where he used scratching techniques to create melodic as well as rhythmic phrases using Fab 5 Freddy's record *Une Sale Histoire (Change the Beat)*. X-Men DJ Rob Swift explains his method of sound manipulation to create a melody via turntables:

> I was watching a DMC tape and there was a DJ on stage doing his routine and one part of his routine consisted of him playing a record that was skipping. I saw that and I was like, wow, imagine where else you could take that idea to. I was playing ... "Public Enemy No 1" record, the 12", just playing it, and what stuck out in my head was that "waahh" sound from the "Blow Your Head" sample that was continuous. Then I started playing with the pitch-control on the turntable while the record was playing and I was like, wow, there's a little melody here. If I left the pitch alone it wouldn't create that melody ... Then it hit me that on the instrumental side it starts with the buzz by itself, then the beats come in. So I'd be doing the melody, but then the beat would come in. The buzz wasn't long enough. So I thought that if I made the record skip on purpose, if I get a piece of tape or scratch it, I could make it skip so that the buzz was continuous. I put a piece of tape on the perfect spot on the groove and it kept skipping. After

a couple of trial and error sessions I got it with the right beat and it's like a sampler. It has drums and it has a groove over it. Back then DJs weren't doing that. They were doing beats, but with actual grooves over them. It was like a bassline that I was playing over it and at the same time breaking a beat down. (Shapiro, 1997, p. 22)

Canadian DJ Kid Koala regards this melodic element of turntablism as being the real testament of the turntable as a musical instrument:

There's all this microtonal stuff and all this sort of tweaking going on which I'm trying to learn how to do ... to blend with other instruments, not just breaks and rhythms. I like to find stuff that's in pitch or that harmonises ... (Shapiro, 1997, p. 24)

Chapter 6

Team Formation and the Creative Processes of Hip-Hop Turntable Teams

Previous chapters have demonstrated how, through the use of sound manipulation techniques such as mixing, beat juggling and scratching, turntable musicians have been able to create original sound material. This chapter will discuss the processes that the hip-hop turntablist teams use to develop this material into an original composition. It will also aim to explore particular notions of creative group work and ways in which these can be applied to the compositional processes of turntable teams.

In order to establish the creative processes of the hip-hop turntable teams, I undertook an empirical examination of the working methods of the three teams using both observation and interview. It became apparent during my examination that similar working methods were being used from team to team. These working methods fell into two areas; the formation and development of each group and the processes involved in the groups' creation of a collective work. Turntable teams such as the Scratch Perverts, the Mixologists and the DMU Crew do not create their compositions from within the western art tradition of an independent artist creating work in isolation, which is then communicated to performers through staff notation. Instead, turntablist teams compose and perform as a collective, creating collaboratively with no use of traditional notation. Within contemporary dance and theatre, this process of a group working collaboratively to create an original work is known as 'devising', a practice that has many similarities to the working methods of hip-hop turntable teams. Because of the great similarities between this devising process and the methods used by the turntable teams, the second half of the chapter will look at a number of devising models to establish which would be most suitable for the analysis of the compositional processes of turntable teams.

Group Formation and Development

In his 1980 book *Organisational Psychology* (cited in Rollinson, Broadfield and Edwards, 1998, pp. 295–6), Schein lists a number of organisational advantages of bringing people together to work in groups. Six of these functions apply directly to the composition work of turntable teams: to work on complex tasks not easily undertaken by an individual; as a means of stimulating creativity and generating new ideas; for problem solving purposes; in situations where multiple viewpoints are important; to fulfil social needs; to establish and test beliefs and experience;

and to achieve mutually agreed informal aims and objectives. Tuckman's staged model of group development, established in 1965 and developed further in 1977 (cited in Rollinson, Broadfield and Edwards, 1998, pp. 301–3), suggests that a group has to pass through a number of stages before it functions effectively. The first stage, 'forming', sees individuals within the group getting to know each other better and trying to create a personal impression. Members get a feel for the roles they would like to play in the group and take part in some degree of task focus. The second stage, 'storming', takes the form of individuals beginning to give their opinion once they know each other better. Polarised views come into the open and differences that arise are resolved through discussion. 'Norming', the third stage of group development, is characterised by task focus and the group clarifies their goals and methodology. Informal codes of conduct are established and distinct roles emerge. 'Performing', the fourth stage, sees structures and procedures put in place and the group is able to focus fully on the task, benefiting from the knowledge and understanding gained during former stages. The work and social functioning of the group begin to complement each other and the group is equipped to perform the task effectively. The final stage, 'adjourning', takes the form of the disbandment of the group either through departure of individuals or completion of the task and is characterised by sadness and anxiety partly due to nostalgic reflection about the work of the group and its members.

These stages of group development are reflected by Michael Farrell (2001) in his book *Collaborative Circles*, which focuses on the work of artistic groups. He describes artists working within such a framework as forming a 'collaborative circle' (p. 7) within which peers share similar artistic goals and develop a common artistic vision through an exchange of support and ideas (p. 266). In his study of collaborative circles Farrell suggests that the development of such a group falls into seven distinct stages, the first five of which are relevant to my study of the composition work of turntablist teams; formation, rebellion against authority, negotiating a new vision, creative work, collective action, separation and nostalgic reunion. As the last two stages refer to the team after the creative work has taken place, I shall not include them in this discussion.

Collaborative Circles

Farrell regards collaborative circles as combining the dynamics of a friendship group and a work group. Circles progress from friendships based on artistic similarities and gradually develop in importance, from playing a minor part in the creative work of the individual members to being a major focus. Through discussions, members cultivate and clarify an artistic standpoint, developing common attitudes and language and through skill sharing, share and expand new techniques. Communication takes place freely and easily as the existing friendship between group members means no new relationships have to be built.

Stage 1: Formation

The turntable teams the Scratch Perverts, the Mixologists and the DMU Crew all developed from friendships based on artistic similarities. Tony Vegas, DJ with the Scratch Perverts, describes how during his childhood all his peers took part in hip-hop culture either through music, breakdancing or graffiti art and explains how his own interest in DJing developed from his participation in the culture as a whole. While working at the record shop 'Mr Bongo', Tony Vegas began to form the team including DJs First Rate, Mr Thing, Renegade, Prime Cuts, Harry Love and beatbox musician Killa Kella. Many of these DJs were already known to each other both socially and professionally. Prime Cuts, admired by Tony Vegas, had known First Rate for many years as they had started DJing at the same time and moved in the same artistic circles (Wax Factor, 1999). Prime Cuts had got to know Tony Vegas through 'Mr Bongo' where Tony Vegas had introduced him to audio tapes of innovative scratching, re-igniting his interest in the genre. DJ Harry Love also met Vegas through the record shop and the pair developed an informal mentoring relationship, practising together. Harry Love comments how Tony Vegas helped him to develop as a DJ and how through Vegas, Harry Love was able to form relationships with the other DJs (Acyde). This mentoring relationship is also evident between the whole Scratch Perverts team and turntablist DJ Plus One, who comments how the team got him in 'the circles' and acknowledges how much he is indebted to them (United DJs). For members of collaborative circles who begin their career within the group, like DJ Plus One, Farrell sees the group as shaping their professional identities through offering an 'informal socialisation' into the discipline (2001, p. 12), developing understanding, orienting them to the main artistic debates and introducing them to the social structure and career ladder.

In a similar way to the formation of the Scratch Perverts, the Mixologists were formed through a desire to bring together a group of like-minded DJs (wildstyle-network.com). DJ Go, the group founder, met fellow team member Beni G when he appeared as a guest on Beni G's radio show 'The Boombox'. And after working with other DJs the pair finally formed the Mixologists with the two final members Gizroc and Yo-One, who they had met through DJ battles (Zaid). DJ Go and Beni G were both raised in London and shared similar influences, admiring the work of the American turntable team the Invisibl Scratch Piklz. Both also shared similar reasons for their own artistic work, citing a love of music as their main impetus for DJing.

For Tony Vegas, the friendship between members is central to the success of the Scratch Perverts:

> You're trying to develop a relationship, the kind of solidarity you would have with the kinship of friends and with family. You want that kind of closeness … Scratch Perverts right now has it as a crew because Prime's one of my best friends and so's Plus One. We have a strength there in friendship, so your ideas and your desire to give a little is more. (Tony Vegas)

Indeed, Beni G goes so far as to regard the whole UK hip-hop scene as 'like a family … Everyone knows everyone' (Felipe, 2001). In discussion about the formation of the Perverted Allies, a turntable team consisting of two members of the Scratch Perverts and two members of the American turntable team The Allies, Vegas comments how the collaboration between the rival teams was a direct result of their developing friendship:

> Off stage we realised we really got along … we developed mutual respect, which developed into friendship, then ultimately a desire to get together and create together. (J.P., 2003)

He goes on to describe how the relationship continues due to a friendship based on similar goals and ambitions, an opinion shared by DJ Plus One who comments about his work with the Scratch Perverts, 'We're just friends and we get along and stuff … we make music together, scratch … just have fun …' (United DJs).

Like the Scratch Perverts and the Mixologists, members of the DMU Crew knew each other professionally and socially before the team was set up and friendship links were already strong. Tim acknowledged how important it was for all members of the team to work with people they 'got along' with and explained that turntable work requires a certain amount of coordination and unspoken communication between musicians, that it is reliant on the relationships between individuals in the group (DMU Crew, 2003).

As in Farrell's first period of formation, this early stage in the development of turntable teams sees the groups begin to cultivate and clarify an artistic standpoint, developing common attitudes and language. Tony Vegas comments how although the Scratch Perverts were intended to include the best turntable musicians it was of great importance that no individual was bigger than the team (Acyde). All members were committed to being part of the team, as DJ Plus One comments, ' … the Scratch Pervert thing was something that started for all the right reasons … it was always a good thing. Everyone's love for it was massive' (United DJs). A clear direction for the team was established by Tony Vegas and Prime Cuts, Vegas explaining during an interview for the BBC how their life experience led to a great sense of clarity regarding their artistic standpoint and direction. In an interview with turntablink.com Vegas commented:

> It was never a point of us considering our opinion on where the Scratch Perverts should go to be more worthy than anybody else's. It was the fact that we were the only two who had an opinion where the Scratch Perverts should go and the joy that going there could bring you. We were the only two who thought about that. (J.P., 2003)

For the DMU Crew, common artistic ground was established early in group formation, as members had worked together previously. In their DJing work, Tim and Adam had played consecutive sets and had a reputation as turntable partners

(DMU Crew, 2003). Both worked as drum and bass DJs in South London and this common artistic ground was enhanced by shared backgrounds and influences. Jon and Tim had also established common artistic ground prior to the establishment of the team, working together informally in the rehearsal studio (DMU Crew, 2003).

Farrell regards the allocation of roles as an intrinsic part of this formation period, each member being assigned an informal role within the group. The importance of role allocation early in the groups' development is mirrored by Rollinson, Broadfield and Edwards in their discussion of group structures in relation to business organisations. The stable and expected patterns of behaviour that arise from clearly defined roles is seen by Rollinson, Broadfield and Edwards as being essential for the development of an effective, cohesive group (1998, p. 316). In *The Presentation of Self in Everyday Life* (1971) Goffman describes how in playing roles, people are 'trading performances' (Rollinson, Broadfield and Edwards, 1998, p. 309) as each individual, aware of the requirements of his or her role and of the roles of the other members, can respond appropriately, thus benefiting the group through the interplay of different patterns of complementary skills and abilities within the group. Roles are allocated according to both functional factors such as the individuals' ability to perform given tasks, status, influence and authority, and personal factors such as personality, attitude, skills and ability (ibid.). The Scratch Perverts, the Mixologists and the DMU Crew all allocated roles to individual members during this period of group formation. Prime Cuts from the Scratch Perverts describes how in early practice sessions team members find their role, testing their relationship with the rest of the team:

> ... when you're trying to put together a crew of DJs, there is actually, initially, quite a bit of ego to overcome, in that, you know, "so-and-so thinks he's the better one" or "so-and-so thinks he's better than so-and-so" and it does take a bit of time to get all that out of the way. (Wax Factor, 1999)

Prime Cuts describes how the team was not directed by a single person commenting, '... that's just not going to happen. I don't think that's any way to work musically when you've got four people trying to come up with something' (Wax Factor, 1999). However, Harry Love, an early member of the Scratch Perverts, describes how although the team was not led by a dominant member, Tony Vegas, as the group's initiator, had a greater say than the other members (Acyde). Prime Cuts makes the distinction between the role of musician and role of visionary, seeing a definite distinction between the kinds of input made by group members:

> Everybody put an equal amount of effort in, but not necessarily everybody put the right amount of effort into thinking about the future and where this thing would go and that was more important than how many hours a day we spent on turntables ... a lot more important. (Acyde)

Though clear that they did not direct or lead the team in any formal way, Tony Vegas and Prime Cuts did consider themselves as the driving force behind the Scratch Perverts regarding both the development of ideas and the practical application of these ideas on turntables.

At the formation of the Mixologists, DJ Go deliberately looked to include DJs who between themselves could fill a variety of roles, including producers, radio DJs, club DJs and mixtape DJs, to widen the artistic possibilities of the team (Zaid). For example, although team member Yo-One was technically proficient he was not musically creative, so his role was to perform the routines that were created by Beni G and DJ Go. Beni G explains how the different roles are shared since Yo-One left the team and how these are taken into account when creating a routine:

> We both make the routines together and we share the good bits and the bad bits as well – some boring bits and some better bits and some bits that I'm better at and some bits that he's better at and bear all that in mind basically when we're doing it. (Beni G, 2002)

Following their formation, the DMU Crew assigned roles according to the strengths and weaknesses of each group member. These roles also reflect non-musical skills of members including leadership skills (DMU Crew, 2003).

Stage 2: Rebellion against Authority

Farrell's second stage of the development of a collaborative circle is the rebellion against authority and, linked to this, collaborative circles as delinquent gangs. A characteristic of this stage is the way in which the group sets itself a position against the established authority of the artistic field. Common ground is established through the group's rejection of the work and attitudes of the establishment and creativity is encouraged to be provocative, the resulting work often taking the form of the vandalism of revered works of the previous generation (Farrell, 2003, p. 14). Farrell describes the group members as 'deviant innovators', who by setting themselves as a group against established rules and procedures, develop an alternative sub-culture based around their shared theory and methodology (ibid., p. 270). For all three turntable teams, the development of either new material or new techniques is of great importance. Tony Vegas describes how at the time of the Scratch Perverts' formation, success was reliant on the ability to deliver something different from the other teams (J.P., 2003). As Plus One comments, their style was more about being able to offer something different than solely being technically good, believing that a recognisable style would separate the team from the other artists (United DJs). Beni G describes innovation as the prime focus of the Scratch Perverts:

> Their sort of innovation and their attitude – they'll look at the turntables and be, rather than … what sounds shall we use, they'll be like how can we mess with the equipment? How can we mess with this to make it completely different? To me, that's crazy good, to keep pushing it in that way. (Beni G, 2002)

Innovation is also a focus for the Mixologist team, Beni G describing the importance of constantly attempting to push boundaries to avoid artistic stagnation. Striving to be different has led the group to use sounds from a wide range of sources not traditionally utilized by hip-hop turntablist teams, for example the use of Drum and Bass and Garage records in their routine for the 2001 DMC team championships (Beni G, 2003). In the DMU Crew, searching for original material often led to the development of new manipulation techniques (DMU Crew, 2003).

The teams' drive to be different to other artists is what Farrell would regard as a quality of a delinquent gang, a characteristic of this second phase of the formation of a collaborative circle. Prime Cuts describes this competitive ethic at the core of the Scratch Perverts' work:

> It's this need to take someone out, to do better than them … I want to do something better than that – it's that mentality that drives us, we want to take on something that we've heard someone else do and try to do it better. (ukhh.com)

The Scratch Perverts' ongoing search for new styles and different approaches to turntable music fits well with Farrell's second-phase characteristic of provocative creativity, a tendency that has been with Tony Vegas since his earliest turntable use:

> The first time I approached a turntable it was always to scratch rather than a fascination with sticking a record on. I just wanted to mess with it! (J.P., 2003)

This early experimentation developed into an even greater provocative form of creativity in the work of the Scratch Perverts. In their collaboration with The Allies for the 2001 DMC team championship the team performed a section of the routine without using records, instead using the turntables and mixers to create the sound. The team created feedback loops using the mixer to create a buzz, from which Prime Cuts made a rhythmic pattern by tapping his finger on the end of a lead attached to the mixer. Rhythms were also built up from sounds generated by letting the needle run against the metal base of the platter and by hitting the needle either on the base of the platter or the central spike. As Plus One describes, it gave the routine a 'bizarre edge' by using sounds that '… would really upset most people if they happened on their stereo' (wildstyle-network.com).

Both the Scratch Perverts and the Mixologists set themselves apart from current trends in the turntable music establishment by questioning the label of 'turntablism' or 'turntablist'. Beni G, whilst accepting that his team is part of the larger turntablist movement regards the term as restricting the possibilities of turntable music. Tony Vegas also acknowledges the turntable musicians' needs for a wider recognition that may result from the use of the umbrella term, but adds:

> The worst thing, also, that could happen to it is that it gets pigeon-holed and it gets categorized … I mean it's turntablism in some people's eyes, in my eyes it's just music. (Vegas)

Stage 3: Negotiating a New Vision

Negotiating a new vision is the third stage of Farrell's development of a collaborative circle, individual members working as a group through discussion and experimentation to establish the beliefs and practices, theory and methodology behind the group's innovative and alternative artistic practice. In the development of this shared vision Farrell regards the group as providing a support structure within which members can explore 'deviant ideas' (2003, p. 271). He suggests that the development of innovative artistic visions is best served through collaborative circles where peers can validate the experiments of individual members, encouraging, supporting and developing (ibid., p. 266) as well as providing support to cope with rejection (ibid., p. 271). This view that some groups offer greater potential for 'risky' experimental and innovative work than people working independently is referred to in group effectiveness theory as 'Group Polarisation' or 'Risky Shift', a phenomenon first described by Stoner in 1961 (Rollinson, Broadfield and Edwards, 1998, p. 318). Rollinson, Broadfield and Edwards cite three reasons for the tendency of groups to develop more innovative work than individuals. Firstly, as group decisions are made, no individual can be blamed if they are wrong. Secondly, risky alternatives have a degree of social prestige and risk takers are seen as dynamic and adventurous. Thirdly, risk starts to look less risky when it is discussed in the group and members become accustomed to it (ibid., pp. 318–19). These elements together create the ideal environment for an innovative approach.

The Scratch Perverts' negotiation of a new vision developed from Tony Vegas' desire to form a team that was better than all other existing teams and that would win the world title. Once the group was formed, this initial idea was developed through discussion and experimentation to establish the theory and methodology of the team in greater detail:

> It felt really strong, it felt that you had a group of people around you that loved the same thing with the same passion and wanted to see the same things … (Vegas)

Although discussions were open to the whole group, it was mostly Tony Vegas and Prime Cuts who took part and therefore became the driving force behind the team in relation to both the generation of ideas and their practical application:

> My major disappointment was that whenever we would bring things together on a major basis it would only ever be myself and Tony that would have input into where we saw this thing going, not just in terms of ideas but we had a five year vision as it were. (Prime Cuts, in Acyde)

Tony Vegas comments how he considers himself and Prime Cuts as the members of the team best placed to expand and develop the artistic vision, explaining how important this developmental input is:

> I would sooner work with a thinker than a grafter 'coz you get grafters to do the work but you need the thought first. (Acyde)

The Scratch Perverts' vision was to develop new artistic practices for turntable music. This desire for originality began early in Tony Vegas' career:

> There got to a point when I wanted to do everybody's patterns and wanted to be the same as everybody but after a while when I started growing older and developing my own sound, to hell with them – their influence was left at the front door and I took over when I got to my room. (Vegas)

The process of developing an artistic vision also happened gradually for Beni G who comments in an interview with the BBC (Beni G, 2001) that his innovative style grew naturally from learning turntable manipulation techniques and the development of a personal approach.

For the Scratch Perverts, developing new ideas and achieving goals is the most challenging part of their artistic work and has greater importance than winning competitions. Although finding that coming up with new ideas can be difficult, Prime Cuts explains how for him it is also extremely rewarding:

> ... that to me is the most exciting thing about the Scratch Perverts; when you see us performing you see some new stuff every time, and that is much more important than seeing some three-year old routine. (MajikFist, 2004)

By evolving innovative ways of sound, the Scratch Perverts attempt to discover new sound and approaches to making music (Marcus, 2004). Prime Cuts comments:

> ... that's what for me music is all about, to keep the thing evolving and to keep reinventing and to come up with new ways and ideas of making music. (Marcus)

DJ Plus One regards the originality achieved through their alternative approaches to turntable music and the importance they place on the development of innovative ideas, as central to the Scratch Perverts' style.

The Mixologists' artistic vision also concerns the desire to develop alternative artistic practices and to be different to other teams. Beni G explains:

> When we're making routines we're like, "have people heard stuff like this before
> or put together in a way like this?" We'll be like "let's scrap it or let's change
> it totally" ... we want to be musical but still have that difference sound-wise.
> (Beni G, 2002)

An important focus for both the Mixologists and the Scratch Perverts is that their artistic vision is shared in an accessible manner and that their work is communicated successfully. Both teams aim to make turntable music accessible and bear this in mind when composing their routines. When questioned about the reasons behind his artistic work Beni G responded:

> Educating people to do music, show them stuff on the turntables that they might
> not be able to do, putting sets together in a way that is a representation of us. So
> it's not just about getting up in front of a set of turntables and scratching. (Gee)

The Scratch Perverts and the Mixologists both provide a supportive environment where what Farrell describes as 'deviant ideas' can be shared and developed. For Tony Vegas, the team environment offered a strength and direction and gave the members the opportunity to stand and believe that the team represented something. Tony Vegas acknowledges that team acted as an important support structure:

> There's strength in numbers. Certainly in this country you need people around
> you because whatever you achieve individually there's going to be a hundred
> people that are willing to tear it away from you – it's an English mentality.
> (Vegas)

Stage 4: Creative Work

The fourth phase as outlined by Farrell, the creative work stage, sees group members dividing their time between working alone, working in small groups with other members and working with the group as a whole. For Farrell, the majority of the creative group work, described as the 'collaborative moments' (2003, p. 23) happen in small-group work, often in pairs. The whole group meetings act more as a time to clarify the group vision and to share and discuss solutions to any problems that may arise when working away from the group.

As outlined by Farrell in the fourth stage of his formation of collaborative circles, the Scratch Perverts, Mixologists and DMU Crew divide their creative work between working alone or in small groups and working in a whole group setting. For Tim, from the DMU Crew, the small group work undertaken by himself and Jon gave them a head start in the creative process which could save time, commenting, 'When the others came around and were trying things, we could say we've already tried that and it didn't work!' (DMU Crew, 2003). For all teams, the creative whole-group work of the team is central to their artistic output and reflects their artistic vision. Vegas describes how he finds the process of a group of musicians creating together on turntables as 'new and exhaustless' (Vegas) offering endless ideas and creative opportunities. DJ Plus One agrees:

> Being in a team of DJs is a massively interesting thing. Your doors are open ... you've got three people – that's six hands – you've got three brains there and if you've got three really good brains, ultimately you've got this new opportunity to kind of come up with ideas and melt ideas together into new things. (Plus One)

Prime Cuts describes how individual practice away from the team demonstrates the competitive nature of team members (Wax Factor, 1999). However, rather than seeing this competitiveness as having a negative effect on the creative work of the group he regards it as a positive force, pushing the team members to achieve more:

> You want to be seen as someone who's vital and one of the best in the crew, so that pushes everyone to work hard. (Wax Factor, 1999)

DJ Plus One also acknowledges the competitive edge to the team and the drive that individual practice brings:

> We're always trying to outdo each other ... Even when we're all working towards the same cause, still at the core of it is that energy – I want to make the best tune this week, I want to have the ideas ... (ukhh.com)

For Plus One this manifests itself in practice sessions with Tony Vegas who he refers to as his sparring partner (United DJs). Vegas however, finds practice sessions the most challenging part of DJing due to the high level of motivation needed to continually come up with new material.

Although individual and small group work is central to the creative work of turntable teams, in whole group situations the role of the individual is outweighed by the importance of the group. As the smaller practice groups come together to collectively create work, the team is able to clarify its artistic vision through practical application and offer solutions to and developmental ideas for work undertaken in the small group sessions. In this context, the individual members take their place within the team. Prime Cuts describes how initially there is much individual ego to overcome (Wax Factor, 1999) and early practice sessions consist of competition between team members before they become comfortable with the relationship between being individually creative and fitting in with the other musicians (Vegas). The teams find ways in which they can benefit from each others' talents to create the best performance as a team without trying to outdo each other. DJ Plus One adds:

> I think we've all realised that it's not necessarily just about all ... going on and trying to do the best thing they all can and doing it together. It's like we can

actually start being musicians ... someone's taking a role that's more minimal to another person, someone else is taking quite a heavy role in this one and soon we'll change over, but ultimately we're actually forming a sound like you would a band ... (Plus One)

Many of the members of turntable teams find coming together and working creatively as a whole group an extremely positive experience and regard it as central to the artistic development and success of the team. Mr Thing from the Scratch Perverts explains how he finds it easier to create collectively rather than in isolation:

> I get more of a vibe when I'm working with other people. If I stood on my own practicing all day I'd go mad. I need to get a response from people. When we're rehearsing we've got a thousand ideas we're bouncing off each other all the time. It works really well. (Nova, 2002)

Plus One comments how the team's shared understanding of the artistic vision and their ability to successfully create routines as a collective is due to the amount of time they work on the compositions, both individually and as a group (Plus One). However, Beni G explains how the intensity of long-term collaborative creative work can become overbearing:

> You want to kill each other! Some days when we practice ... we're doing twelve-hour days ... The only way I can explain it is it's like two, three or four artists all holding the same paint brush wanting to paint one picture and they're all trying to paint it in a slightly different way and you've got to compromise in some areas to get your piece, your portrait. It gets horrible ... it's difficult you know. (Beni G, 2002)

However, this process of creating collectively develops and improves with time as members become used to each others working practices and roles. Beni G describes how the awareness of the team's working methods has impacted on their collaborative work, assisted by a shared understanding of the artistic focus:

> Go knows how I work, I know how he works and we know what sounds we want together. We know kind of how we want to do it, we know what we want to do. We've just got common ground, so it's really easy ... We've tailored what we want and how we want to do it and it's easier to do that ... it's kind of easy, the more you work with people. (Beni G, 2003)

Often, work undertaken by individuals and small groups is through necessity rather than choice. The ability for a team to meet up on a regular basis may be affected by the geography or lifestyle of individual members. In the collaboration between the Scratch Perverts and The Allies for example, the time the team had to work creatively together was severely restricted by the location of group members as the Scratch Perverts are based in London and The Allies in Miami.

Stage 5: Collective Action

Farrell regards the fifth stage of the development of a collaborative circle as the collective action stage, the group carrying out a project together. For the first time in its development, the group shifts from the inward preoccupation of the artistic vision and the development and application of the new theory and methodology, to the outward-looking desire to create a completed piece of work and to present the new work of the group to an audience. With this shift in group focus may come an increase in conflict and the roles of the group may change, sometimes resulting in the immergence of a member in an executive role to organise the group and deal with the outside world.

In the collective action stage of collaborative circle formation, turntable teams such as the Scratch Perverts, the Mixologists and the DMU Crew work to create compositions, referred to as 'routines' to be performed live to a public audience, often in a competition (also referred to as a 'battle') or showcase environment. Each routine is collectively composed for a specific performance and is usually performed only once. These routines are entirely composed and rehearsed prior to performance and unlike the club-based performances of turntable teams, do not allow for any improvisation. For turntable teams, this degree of formality alongside the need to create innovative routines that aims to showcase the work of the team and win competitions, leads to a lengthy and intense composition process. For the Mixologists, competitions give the team the opportunity to display their talents in a public arena, performing new routines that have taken hours to create. Beni G explains how this can be an extremely nerve-wracking experience as they have only one opportunity to show themselves at their best. Being successful in competitions is important for the Mixologists, and Beni G describes how the high profile of the competitions offers great opportunities in terms of sponsorship and future work. Although the Scratch Perverts strive to compose the most innovative turntable compositions in order to win competitions, the work of the team and the creation and development of new artistic practices are the first priority. Prime Cuts reflects on what he regards as their unsatisfactory performance at the 2002 DMC World Team Championship competition, commenting '... I'm not that upset because even though we fucked it that night we ran that thing a hundred times in rehearsal perfectly' (Acyde). Indeed, the team's love of creating new and innovative artistic practices has led to criticism as they spend more time developing new material than perfecting its execution, which sometimes impacts on the quality of their performance (MajikFist, 2004).

Like Farrell, the business author Belbin (1981 and 1993, cited in Rollinson, Broadfield and Edwards, 1998, pp. 323–4) suggests ways in which the roles of the individual may change in later stages of the groups' development as the task progresses. Belbin reflects how in smaller groups, members may be allocated more than one role. During the collective action stage roles in the turntable teams may also alter, firstly to ensure that all members are being utilised to their maximum capacity and secondly, as Prime Cuts explains, because some members may be unavailable for the rehearsals or performance, resulting in their roles being shared out among other members.

It is evident that the UK hip-hop turntable teams studied exhibit many characteristics of the group formation of collaborative circles. However, the level of collaboration is often much greater than that outlined by Farrell, existing not only in the formation and development of the group but also in their creative work and artistic output. In Farrell's description of collaborative circles, artists may exchange ideas and support each other's artistic work (the creative work stage) and may even carry out a project together, for example a performance or an exhibition (collective action stage). However, this collective action rarely manifests itself in co-created pieces of work as produced by the turntable teams. For them, the creative work and collective action stages are intertwined and artistic works are produced through a process of collective creation. Through analysing interviews with musicians from turntable teams, it becomes apparent that the compositional process is not regarded as a separate facet of the genre but is seen as a natural extension to practicing and experimenting with sounds and techniques. For hip-hop turntable teams, practice, the acquisition and attainment of skills and techniques related to performance is synonymous with the creation and development of original material, composition. The creation of new music is part of the learning process, not separate from it. As in many popular music genres, turntablists may begin by imitating favourite musicians and experimenting with techniques in order to learn to play their instrument. Learning through imitation and experimentation allows for a development of both manual and technical skills and in hip-hop turntablism this leads quickly to the composition of original material. The reasons for this are two-fold. Firstly, the music of turntable teams is constructed from manipulated parts of records. Unless the young turntablist is fortunate enough to own the same records as owned and used by the recorded artist they will be unable to imitate the track in any great detail. What the young turntablist can imitate however, is the manipulation techniques used on the record such as mixing and scratching – techniques that effect both material and form. The turntablist would use these techniques on the records available, thus developing a personal style and creating original music from the outset. Turntable musicians may incorporate techniques pioneered by other musicians into their routines but they would not want to be seen as imitating or recreating an existing routine. Indeed, the individual style of musicians is of great importance in turntablism. Whereas many classically-trained musicians acquire skills that enable them to perform the work of other composers, hip-hop turntablist musicians learn techniques that enable them to create and perform their own original routines, in the case of turntable teams, within an artistic group.

Devising Processes

In the work of the UK hip-hop turntable teams studied, collaboration occurs within a larger creative framework in which the group members work together to create an original piece of music. In their collective creation the turntablists demonstrate how such collaboration need not be restricted to group formation as in Farrell, but is central to the creative work of the team. Within contemporary dance and theatre the process of collective creation, where a group collaborates together over a period of time to create an original performance, is known as devising. As Sue Gibbons explains in Gill Lamden's book *Devising* (2000):

> It's about ownership, negotiation, compromise, developing and exploring feelings, ideas and philosophies. It's about spontaneity, excitement and originality. It's about the dynamics and chemistry of this group of people at this moment in time, which changes from day to day. (Lamden, 2000, pp. 7–8)

Devised performance originates from within the group rather than relying on an interpretation of an existing text. Alison Oddey (1994) explains how the work is shaped through the group's experimentation with ideas within a pre-determined framework established by the group:

> Devising is about thinking, conceiving and forming ideas, being imaginative and spontaneous as well as planning. It is about inventing, adapting and creating what you do as a group. (1994, p. 1)

To look at the compositional process of turntable teams as involving devising processes does not mean that we must reject the importance of the collaborative circle. Indeed, Torunn Kjølner (2001), Lamden and Oddey all stress the centrality of collaboration in the devising process. Kjølner states that devising is characterised by its reliance on collaborative processes and Oddey cites collaboration as one of the four major elements of devising along with process, multivision and artistic creation (1994, p. 3). Although the collaborative circle outlines the structure in which team turntable music is made, the process of devising may help us to see the process of *how* it is made. Before I can discuss the relevance of devising to the creative process of hip-hop turntable teams it is necessary for me to establish the definitions and characteristics of devising as outlined by the authors Torunn Kjølner (2001), Alison Oddey (1994), Gill Lamden (2000) and Leigh Landy and Evelyn Jamieson (2000).

Devising Frameworks

Torunn Kjølner

For Kjølner (2001), devising is not a rigid structural process reliant on rules and regulations, but rather 'a collection of practices, which have some family resemblances or characteristics' (p. 1). Kjølner regards the devising process as consisting of three distinct phases. In the first phase the artists generate the material, in the second phase the artists select and compose the material and in the third phase the artists rehearse and perform the emerging work. All three phases also include discussion, which Kjølner regards as offering vital analytical reference throughout the creative process (p. 1). Kjølner describes how the devising process is shaped by the different ways that each of the three phases can relate together and offers examples. The first example he gives shows the group of artists spending the majority of the process generating material, organizing their time in phases such as selecting material, rehearsing and revising. In the second example, Kjølner describes the group of artists using exercises and rehearsing as part of generating material, thus building the performance step by step (p. 5).

Alison Oddey

For Oddey (1994), the devising process is unique for each group and its inherent eclecticism makes it impossible to articulate any single theory (p. 2). Oddey characterises devising as having to include four separate elements: process (finding ways to work creatively together), collaboration (working with others), multivision (integrating various views and attitudes) and the creation of the artistic product (p. 3). Although stressing that there is 'no one accepted way of devising a performance', each group generating its own working processes, Oddey does outline 10 guidelines to support the devising process (p. 149):

1. Clearly establish roles and responsibilities;
2. Consider writing a Code of Practice document;
3. If applicable, establish leadership and delegate or form hierarchies according to skills and interests;
4. Have an initial sense of what the group would like to achieve, aim for or create;
5. Trust to feelings and instinct about the development of the work;
6. Allow group members to work on their own sometimes. Consider dividing into smaller groups with specific tasks;
7. Ask questions throughout the process and, if necessary, return to original aims and objectives to clarify direction;
8. Consider space, setting and location;
9. Analyse, criticise, assess and evaluate the work as it progresses;

10. Try to remain critical to the process and product, both on a subjective and objective level.

Oddey also attempts to define the devising process in a four-stage theoretical model (p. 152). Stage 1, entitled 'Pre-production Planning' includes finding the starting stimulus, identifying materials and resources, sharing initial ideas for content, form and audience and defining preliminary boundaries. Stage 2, 'Questioning/ Exploring/Discussing the Preliminary Decision' includes the establishment of aims and objectives, and preliminary discussions take place and decisions made concerning the content, form and structure. During this stage, artists also establish an organisational procedure covering roles, responsibilities and methods of working. All decisions and discussions are made through research, discussion and trying out ideas. Stage 3, 'Examining Specifics of the Decision', involves the artists discussing the initial starting point further, building and developing their initial ideas, making decisions about content and form and creating a more detailed structure for a practical exploration of the chosen stimulus. Stage 4, 'Somewhere in the Process – Difficulties' covers the artists questioning their aims and objectives in relation to the emerging work, the success of individual sections and the success of the work as a whole. Although Oddey presents these elements of the devising process in stages, she stresses that she does not envisage them necessarily following each other chronologically. Rather, she suggests that they form a flexible structure, elements changing order and significance as is necessary, dependent on the needs of the devising group. Like Kjølner, Oddey stresses the importance of identifying and clarifying the groups' intention throughout the process.

Gill Lamden

In her book *Devising* (2000), Gill Lamden dedicates an entire chapter to a model framework of the devising process. She regards devising as an exhausting and constant 'process of decision making and creation' (p. 94) and suggests that the use of an established structure or framework frees some of the energy for making important creative decisions. Lamden divides the devising process into a nine-week schedule, structured to reflect her aim to create a straightforward template for first-time devising students. In the first week of her nine-week plan, Lamden suggests that the devising group focuses on pre-devising administration such as establishing a rehearsal schedule and the resources and technical equipment needed for the project. Lamden regards team-building as an important aspect of this early phase, suggesting that the group establish ground rules as well as determining the skills of individual group members and allocating team functions. According to Lamden this stage should also include the first rehearsals where the team begins to establish objectives and generate and develop its ideas, mostly through practical experimentation rather than discussion. The second week of Lamden's devising model includes the team continuing its research and developing the material generated in the initial rehearsals. At this stage the artists also begin to experiment with different structures. This focus on structure is continued in the third week of devising where Lamden suggests the group develop material for highlighted sections of the piece and begin to run sections, possibly sharing the work with others in order to receive constructive feedback. The development of the material continues throughout stage four of the process, though by week five Lamden suggests that while the group continues experimenting with ideas they should begin to formalise the material within the structure and start to rework sections. Lamden describes how in week six of the process the sections of the piece can begin to be put in a final order, the group running the piece for continuity and timing. Content and complexity is developed and the group begins to rehearse the piece according to feedback. In week seven, the group develops the piece according to any critical feedback received and runs the piece, ensuring that the length is correct. Week eight continues these final rehearsals and also focuses on the transitions between sections, ensuring that all aspects of the performance are well rehearsed and fluid. The artists should also ensure that they have all resources and technical requirements necessary for the performance. The performance week consists of final rehearsals and any last minute changes or developments.

Leigh Landy and Evelyn Jamieson

In *Devising Dance and Music*, Leigh Landy and Evelyn Jamieson (2000) put forward a framework for the devising process. Commenting that a fixed framework contradicts the freedom inherent in the devising process and may result in confinement, they intend the framework to be flexible, allowing groups to decide upon and utilise the aspects that they feel are relevant to their own working contexts. Landy and Jamieson establish six categories within the framework. The first of these categories, entitled, 'Create the working parameters of the group', includes establishing common ground between the artists, deciding what aspect of common ground is to be investigated and how this can be manifested in the work. Also at this stage, the group will establish and begin to investigate a theme or stimulus for the devised work deciding what form this theme may take and what the end product may be. The second category, 'The preliminary workshop takes place – testing the water' focuses on further team-building, the group getting to know each other better but now also beginning to create material. In category three, described by Landy and Jamieson as 'Creation of the storyboard or basic template', the group establishes the best way to share ideas and works towards creating a storyboard or template that reflects the expertise of the artists and the level of flexibility required. Category four, 'Set the first task' concerns the first major practical workshops. Focused workshops are planned, material is generated and the first selections are made. The first evaluations take place and the group discusses the process of selecting and altering material. Ideas are developed and are measured through a comparison with the initial aims. Landy and Jamieson describe category five as 'The devising inner-cycle of development and evaluation'. In this section begins the 'cyclical process' of devising that the authors regard as one of the most exciting aspects of devising – the continual discussion and evaluation of the process. The loop begins with follow-up tasks being set through targeted workshops and results are shared and discussed by the group. The resulting opinions influence further developments, which in turn are re-evaluated. Discussions and resulting developments may focus on any aspect of the devised work, Landy and Jamieson giving examples such as the development of the piece, the quantity of material generated, structure and process. Selections are made of content and structure, possible alterations are discussed and ideas are developed further. Landy and Jamieson explain how this constant cyclical process of discussion, alteration, development and re-evaluation continues in a loop until the work reaches the end of its active life.

Three of the four devising frameworks – those outlined by Kjølner, Oddey and Landy and Jamieson – are intended as flexible frameworks. All four authors highlight the importance of the process being shaped by the devising group who select elements of the process relevant to their working practices and artistic needs. Although Kjølner sets out his framework in phases and Oddey sets out her framework in stages, neither author intends the framework to necessarily be followed chronologically. Landy and Jamieson avoid this assumption by constructing their framework in categories. The framework outlined by Lamden, however, is chronological and is less flexible than those of other authors. She divides the process in weeks, reflecting the fact that her framework was created specifically as a rehearsal schedule model for students new to devising. Although the four frameworks vary in the number of stages, phases, weeks and categories, the content of the frameworks and the elements of the devising process included are similar, though they do differ slightly in order. All authors suggest aspects of establishing the group and working parameters early on in the process, for example establishing common ground, roles and responsibilities and the skills of individual members. All authors outline that the first artistic discussions and early rehearsals should focus on establishing and investigating the nature of the product, outlining aims and objectives, and agreeing on the initial stimulus or theme. At this early stage all authors agree that the devising group should establish parameters for a constructive process, for example setting frameworks for the production of material (Kjølner), establishing how to share ideas (Landy and Jamieson) and drawing and defining preliminary boundaries (Lamden). Ideas and material should begin to be generated and shared. Although the four frameworks are set out differently, the middle stages of the devising processes again show great similarities, including elements such as establishing a basic structure or template, allocating tasks, generating and developing ideas and content, sharing and selecting material, confirming content and sections and reworking. Central to all the devising frameworks is the importance of reflection and evaluation in the process. Throughout all the frameworks, the devising group is encouraged to question decisions on all aspects of the artistic process and the emerging piece. The authors outline that this reflection and evaluation can take place both within the group and also resulting from feedback from any sharings of the work to an audience during the process. Although this aspect of the process is evident in all of the four frameworks, it is most strongly so in that of Landy and Jamieson who formally include it in category five of their devising process, the 'inner cycle of development and evaluation'.

A Devising Framework for the Analysis of Hip-Hop Turntable Teams

To be able to analyse the creative process of hip-hop turntable teams from a devising standpoint it is necessary to compare their creative process with devising models. To assist in this, a model framework of the devising process has been constructed, based on the major elements outlined by Kjølner, Lamden, Oddey and Landy and Jamieson. This framework has been created not to provide a practical detailed template for devising groups to follow, but to enable the identification of any similar patterns in the creative processes of the teams studied:

Table 6.1   Model framework of the devising process

Stage 1	Pre-devising administration	• Team-building • Establishing the working parameters of the group • Allocation of roles • Establish skills of individuals • Establish common artistic ground
Stage 2	Preliminary rehearsals	• Discuss theme and end product • Establish parameters for a constructive process • Generate and share ideas • Create and share material
Stage 3	Rehearsals phase 1	• Establish creative framework • Create basic 'template' for structure • Generate material • Try sections
Stage 4	Rehearsals phase 2 Inner cycle of development and evaluation – the devising loop	• Develop ideas and content • Set and work on individual and group tasks • Share with group • Select and discard material • Confirm content and clarify sections • Reflect and evaluate • Re-work according to feedback
Stage 5	Final rehearsals and performance	• Rehearse and perform

Note: Adapted from Kjølner, Lamden, Landy and Oddey.

Chapter 7
An Analytical Methodology for Hip-Hop Turntable Music

This chapter will aim to produce a suitable analytical methodology for the study of the composition processes of hip-hop turntable teams and will be structured in three main sections. The first section will look at some existing analytical methodologies for hip-hop and popular music in general, discussing their suitability for an analysis of team turntablism. The second section will focus on frameworks for the analysis of hip-hop turntable music and the development of a new analytical model. The final section will explore emerging notation and transcription techniques and, following a discussion of the implication and use of such systems, set out a notational system for the analysis of specific turntable team compositions.

Analytical Methodologies

Joseph Schloss, in his book *Making Beats* (2004), undertakes a study of hip-hop composition that focuses on the creative practices of hip-hop composition in a studio context. Schloss highlights a number of difficulties in finding a suitable existing methodology for the analysis of hip-hop. Academic literature around the genre has tended to emerge from a variety of disciplines and many have been orientated towards a sociological or textual analysis which results in an 'unbalanced' analytical focus (2004, p. 21).

In *Capturing Sound* (2005) Mark Katz does provide an analysis a piece of hip-hop turntable music – I. Emerge's winning routine from the 2003 World Series Turntable Championships. This is a thorough analysis of the two-minute hip-hop turntable composition, Katz commenting that he hopes such a detailed analysis will make such complex routines easier to follow, increasing understanding and appreciation of the genre (ibid., p. 128). However, Katz's analysis takes a chronological approach, and whilst this is appropriate for a composition created and performed by a single musician it is not so suitable for the analysis of team compositions, where aspects need to be compared thematically.

Much academic literature concerning popular music has focused on the interrelationships between society and music and the ways in which social meaning is produced (Susan McClary and Robert Walser, 2000, p. 281) resulting in what Simon Frith regards as a pre-occupation with 'sociology rather than sound' (cited in Roy Shuker, 2001, p. 140). Philip Tagg goes as far as to describe musicological content analysis as the 'missing link' (2000, p. 74) and for authors McClary and Walser this neglect of musical components in favour of sociological aspects is 'the greatest single failure of musicology' (2000, p. 286). Numerous frameworks and methodologies for the analysis of popular music have been developed but have failed to grow into a definitive school of thought and have remained instead, a 'collection of intriguing and highly suggestive fragments ...' (McClary and Walser, 2000, p. 275).

The lack of any dominant framework or methodology for the musicological analysis of popular music has created a 'methodological vacuum' (ibid., p. 281) in which musicologists must often develop their own techniques from scratch before any analysis can take place. To address the lack of academic work that deals with the actual music of hip-hop culture, I aim to establish a methodology that values the creative process and supports its analysis rather than using a sociological analysis. To assist in the development of such a musicology I have drawn on the work of Jean-Jacques Nattiez (1990). Although Nattiez is not a scholar of popular music, the value he places on the role of the creative process in musicology is extremely relevant to my focus.

In the introduction to his book *Music and Discourse* (1990), Nattiez sets forward his hypothesis that a musical work cannot be simply understood as an autonomous text, a whole composed of 'structures', but is constituted by the procedures that engendered it (acts of composition) and procedures to which it gave rise (acts of interpretation and perception) (ibid., p. xi). Nattiez outlines three categories, corresponding to three families of analysis, that he regards as defining this 'total musical fact' (ibid., p. xi); the immanent level (the 'material reality' of the work, for example the score [ibid., p. 12]), the esthesic level (the 'engaging, contemplating or reading' of a musical performance (ibid., p. 12) and, most relevant to my study, the poietic level. Nattiez defines the poietic level as the 'process of creation' from which music results (ibid., p. 12) and his outline of the level's main characteristics and areas for analysis offers a model for the process-focused methodology required by my study. Gilson, who first used the term in his book *Introduction aux Arts du Beau* (1963), regarded every artistic work as the product of an act of making:

> Gilson understood the determination of the conditions that make possible, and that underpin the creation of an artist's (or a producer's or an artisan's) work – thanks to which something now exists which would not have existed, except for them. (Nattiez, 1990, p. 13)

Gilson divides the poietic level into three elements; deliberations on what must be done to produce the object, operations upon external materials and the production of the work. In his article 'Esquisse d'une semiologie de la poesie' (1984), Molino redefines Gilson's field of inquiry demonstrating how poietics is applicable to poetry, though to demonstrate the pertinence of the definition for my analysis I have replaced references to poetry with non arts-specific references:

(1) the study of techniques and rules which, at a given moment, for a given form, define the state of the resources and procedures used by the [artist] (for example the techniques …); (2) analysis of particular strategies of production which, from evidence and clues left by the [artist], or from characteristics of the work itself, serve to furnish a model for the production of the work …; (3) study of the intention of the [artist], who in the plastic arts or in literature often wants to communicate or express something about the work … (Adapted from Molino, 1984, pp. 9–10)

The importance of including the creative process in an analysis of music is stressed by both Gilson and Molino who, between them, offer four areas of focus for a poietic reading:

1. deliberations on what must be done to produce the music;
2. the intention of the artist;
3. a study of techniques and operations upon external materials;
4. procedures used by the artist and strategies of production, which may offer a model for the production of the work.

Molino suggests that these areas can be approached in two ways; firstly by analysing evidence left by the artist who, he reflects, often want to express or communicate something about the work and secondly through an analysis of the music itself. Schloss (2004), in his study of hip-hop composition, also comes to the conclusion that the aesthetics of hip-hop composition are best studied through a methodology based around participant observation and interviews:

> This is especially valuable in the case of hip-hop, as the culture's participants have invested a great deal of intellectual energy in the development of elaborate theoretical frameworks to guide its interpretation. (Schloss, 2004, p. 6)

Schloss feels such issues are better addressed through the discourse of hip-hop musicians than solely through the objective analysis of specific musical texts (2004, p. 13), criticising hip-hop musicologists for focusing on the results of composition rather then the process (2004, p. 20). My own methodology reflects this belief in the importance of first-hand research within the hip-hop community through observation of the teams and discussion with team musicians, an approach that sits well with a poietic analysis which by its nature is reliant on the artists having spoken about their work (Nattiez, 1990, p. 4). Unlike Schloss, however, my research also requires Molino's second analytical approach, an analysis of the music itself.

Analysis Frameworks

To fully explore the compositional processes in relation to the completed work I also require a more in-depth analysis of the music itself. The methodologies of Philip Tagg (2000), Stan Hawkins (2002), Allan Moore (2001) and Tim Wall (2003) offer some useful approaches that can be applied to an analysis of hip-hop team compositions. In his article 'Analysing Popular Music: Theory, Method and Practice', Tagg offers a six-part analytical model, the first element of which – the 'checklist of parameters of musical expression' – is pertinent for any analysis of popular music. In it, Tagg outlines seven musical aspects; aspects of time, melodic aspects, orchestrational aspects, aspects of tonality and texture, dynamic aspects, acoustical aspects and electromusical and mechanical aspects. He advises that the checklist should be used flexibly, as a guideline to ensure that no important parameters of musical expression are overlooked in analysis:

Table 7.1   Tagg's 'Checklist of parameters of musical expression'

1	Aspects of time	Duration of analysis object and relation of this to any other simultaneous forms of communication; Duration of sections within the analysis object; Pulse, tempo, metre, periodicity; Rhythmic texture and motifs.
2	Melodic aspects	Register; Pitch range; Rhythmic motifs; Tonal vocabulary; Contour; Timbre.
3	Orchestrational aspects	Type and number of voices, instruments, parts; Technical aspects of performance; Timbre; Phrasing; Accentuation.
4	Aspects of tonality and texture	Tonal centre and type of tonality (if any); Harmonic idiom; Harmonic rhythm; Type of harmonic change; Chordal alteration; Relationships between voices, parts, instruments; Compositional texture and method.
5	Dynamic aspects	Levels of sound strength; Accentuation; Audibility of parts.
6	Acoustical aspects	Characteristics of (re-)performance 'venue'; Degree of reverberation; Distance between sound source and listener; Simultaneous 'extraneous' sound.
7	Electromusical and mechanical aspects	Panning, filtering, compressing, phasing, distortion, delay, mixing, etc.; Muting, pizzicato, tongue flutter, etc. (see 3, above).

Source: Middleton, 2000a, p. 82.

Hawkins similarly outlines five types of basic musical elements which he feels should be acknowledged in any analysis, referring to these categories as 'basic types of compositional features' (2002, pp. 11–12); formal properties, harmonic idioms, recording and production techniques, textures and timbres and rhythmic syntax:

Table 7.2   Hawkins' 'Basic types of compositional features'

1	Formal properties	The sections within the song's overall structure, often binary, that support the general progression of technical codes.
2	Harmonic idioms	The goal-directed or static progressions depending on genre and style, harnessing tonal or modal systems.
3	Recording and production techniques	The controlling function of the production as manifested in the audio mix, which is responsible for shaping the compositional design.
4	Textures and timbres	The heterogeneous profusions of colours and patterns that arise from vocal and instrumental gestures within the arrangement.
5	Rhythmic syntax	The recurring groupings and combinations of metric patterns that communicate the 'beat', groove and 'feel' of the text.

Source: Hawkins, 2002, pp. 11–12.

For Hawkins, stylistic and technical codes such as socio-cultural factors and music-theoretical parameters slot into these compositional features, blending, into the compositional design. Moore, in his analytical framework, favours a 'stratified layer model' (2001, p .33), which divides the analysis into four relatively discrete layers; the rhythmic layer, the deepest notes, the higher frequency melodies and the harmonic filler:

Table 7.3   Moore's 'Stratified layer model'

1	Rhythmic layer	Precise pitch is irrelevant; layer is preserve of the drum kit and other percussion.
2	The deepest notes (those with lowest frequency)	Can be thought of as a low register melody; normally restricted to the bass guitar.
3	Higher frequency melodies	Either sung or played by a variety of instruments; corresponds to the common-sense understanding of 'tune'.
4	Harmonic filler	Fills the registeral gap between the second and third layers by supplying harmonies congruent to each of these. The instruments can vary and can include voices.

Source: Moore, 2001, p. 33.

Although the basic elements are distinguishable from each other in abstract, Moore reflects that such analytical reduction is useful only if the elements are reconstructed at a later stage of the analysis, giving an opportunity to understand how the layers work together to create the music we hear (2001, p. 32). Wall (2003) also offers a framework of musical elements to be considered in analysis. This model places Moore's stratified layers within an instrumental category, which also covers the roles of the musicians and descriptions of form, and includes two additional categories of vocal style and recording techniques:

Table 7.4   Wall's 'Elements for analysing popular music meanings'

1	Instrumentation	The way the group of musicians is organised/The instruments musicians play/The roles the musicians take.
		Examining 4 levels of musical organisation (Moore, 2001, pp. 31–55):
		a. Rhythmic – the drum kit and percussion.
		b. Low-register melody – usually the bass guitar.
		c. Higher frequencies – a variety of instruments, forming the 'tune'.
		d. Harmonic filler – instruments adopting sonic places between levels 2 and 3.
		The descriptions of form produced through the analysis must then be related to the interpretations made by listeners.
2	Vocal style	Four qualities to be analysed (Moore):
		a. Register and range – the height and spread of the voice's pitch.
		b. Resonance – the thin voice resonating in the nose against the full resonance in the chest.
		c. Deviations from tempered pitches – including slides and slurs of notes.
		d. Attitude to rhythm – including anticipation and delay, stress and accenting within beats.
		It can also be applied to the distinctive styles of instrumental players.

3	Recording techniques	Qualities of recording that give particular records their distinctive style. Even though much popular music analysis is based on listening to records, there has been almost no analysis of the process used to produce the musical recording. A basic analysis would involve examining four main factors:
		a. Mic-ing/sampling – The way that voices and instruments are converted into an electrical signal. The acoustics of the recording space. The distance of the voice/instrument from the microphone. The source of the sound. b. Recording – The way that the electrical signals are stored e.g. direct to disc or tape. The number of tracks recorded. The ways to layer sound (e.g. through digital recording). c. Mixing – The relative volume of different sound signals in the recording. d. Degree of overt production – The degree to which techniques and quality of mic-ing, multi-tracking and mixing dominate the textural qualities. The way in which the production has given the music a distinctive sound (for example, Jamaican dub reggae and computer-produced dance music).

Source: Wall, 2003, pp. 136–8.

Wall recommends this analytical approach for comparing the distinctive sound and styles of one recording against another but does suggest that the model can be applied to a single recording, to the work of one artist or to a genre of music as a whole.

These models offer firm frameworks for the analysis of popular music and succeed in shedding the 'hidden ideological claptrap' that McClary and Walser see as being inherent in musicological training (2000, p. 281). Traditional musicology, they suggest, locates value and meaning in aspects of pitch and harmony yet in popular music the interest often lies elsewhere. These frameworks address this problem, giving equal importance to aspects such as texture, performance style acoustics and recording and production techniques, elements that are often overlooked by traditional musicology. Although these frameworks offer a more suitable approach to the analysis of popular music in general, to what extent can they be used for an exploration of the creative parameters specific to hip-hop turntable music? All of the approaches discussed above manifest two major assumptions inappropriate to hip-hop turntablism. Firstly, the frameworks tend to reflect the authors' focus on popular music in song form, for example Tagg's (1991) analysis of Abba's song *Fernando* and Hawkins' analysis of songs by Madonna, Morrissey, Annie Lennox, The Pet Shop Boys and Prince (2002). Whilst offering the analytical parameters such as acoustics and individual performance style, the frameworks still concentrate on aspects that relate mainly to song form, such as lyrics, melody, harmonic progression and song structure, that are not necessarily appropriate to an instrumental or non-vocal style of music such as hip-hop turntablism. Secondly, the majority of the frameworks include recording as a category for analysis, not suitable for this study that focuses on the creation of music primarily intended for live performance. The inclusion of these categories in the frameworks poses no great problem for my analysis as Tagg advises that his parameters are intended as a guideline only and, as such, some aspects can be discarded. However, as well as including parameters that are not relevant to hip-hop turntable music, the frameworks also omit many aspects central to it, such as the choice and use of samples and the use of sound manipulation techniques. In order to deal with these inconsistencies, a framework has been formed through which to undertake an analysis of hip-hop team turntablism composition. Whilst being based on the models outlined above, it omits irrelevant categories and includes additional aspects central to an understanding of the genre and its music:

Table 7.5   Framework for the analysis of hip-hop team turntable composition

1	Context	Any relevant background information.
2	The process of collective creation	Through five-stage devising framework established in Chapter 4: Pre-devising administration. Preliminary rehearsals. Rehearsals phase 1. Rehearsals phase 2. Final rehearsals and performance.
3	Group organisation	Number of parts. Instruments/equipment. Roles of individuals.
4	General properties	Duration of routine and sections within it. Pulse, tempo and metre.
5	Sample choice (instrumentation)	Instrumental samples. Vocal samples. Sound effects and any other samples.
6	Structure	Form of sections within the composition.
7	Sound manipulation techniques	Mixing, punchphasing and backspinning, scratching, beat juggling, pitch alteration. Any other techniques specific to individual teams. Allocation of manipulation techniques.

8	Texture	Relationships between parts.
		Perceived foreground and background.
		Audibility of parts.
		Levels of sound strength and relative volume.

This framework fuses the approaches of popular musicologists such as Katz, Tagg, Hawkins, Moore and Wall with the poietic methodology of Nattiez. It shares Katz's focus on sample choice, sound manipulation techniques, structure and texture, but blends these with Nattiez's two other analytical categories – the immanent (in the creation and use of a score of the finished routines) and the aesthesic (in the description of the work itself). While providing an analytical model that relates to a more formal analysis of music including elements such as tempo, form and instrumentation it also facilitates a process-based analysis covering group organisation, sound manipulation techniques and creative process. Such a dual-focused approach offers a framework that meets all the aims of my analysis.

To explore the artistic parameters of turntable team compositional process as outlined in my analytical framework, it was necessary to clearly establish the way in which the techniques and roles of individuals have come together through chosen procedures to create a finished artistic product. To do this, not only must the process be evidenced, but it must also show how these aspects are manifested in the finished work. The parameters of the framework can be explored through methods such as interviews, participant observation and watching the video-documented performances of the finished compositions, but it is much more useful for the purpose of the analysis to also have a static documentation achieved through notation. Nattiez sees transcriptions as being central to any multi-faceted analysis of a work (Nattiez, 1990, p. 72) and even Schloss, who rejects notation as a suitable analytical method in his own work, acknowledges its use in objectifying the results of musical processes to highlight specific elements 'that could not be presented as clearly through other means' (Schloss, 2004, p. 12).

Chapter 8
Notation and Transcription Techniques

Many popular musicologists are wary of using notation as an analytical tool for two main reasons. Firstly, popular music is rarely notated from its conception, its primary medium of transmission being recording. As such, it is neither conceived nor designed to be stored or distributed as notation (Tagg, 2000 p. 75). Secondly, the traditional staff notation is often unsuitable for transcribing much popular music. Tagg describes how many of the most important parameters of musical expression are difficult or even impossible to transcribe using such notation (ibid., p. 75). This leads to an over-emphasis on features that can be notated easily at the expense of others (Middleton, 2000a, p. 4) and elements such as pitch, melody and harmony are given priority at the expense of elements such as texture, timbre and sound manipulation, which are seen as of secondary importance (Moore, 2001, p. 15). Schloss (2004) highlights previous transcriptions of hip-hop (citing Walser (1995), Gaunt (1995), Keyes (1996) and Krims (2000)) which approach notation through the conceptual frameworks of European art music and in doing so prioritise the transcription of pitches and rhythms, the separation of individual instruments in score form and linear development. While he does not question the accuracy and significance of these transcriptions, he suggests that they offer a particular perspective which pushes many of the characteristics central to hip-hop composition into second place or omits them completely (Schloss, 2004, p. 14). Schloss chooses to undertake his analysis of sample-based hip-hop without notating many musical examples. Only two short excerpts are transcribed, depicted in a matrix editor format similar to that in sequencer software used by the artists he studied. The transcriptions are used to demonstrate the transformations made on a sampled bass line using the techniques of chopping and re-arranging (ibid., p. 108). Schloss's avoidance of notation is a clear choice and reflects his belief that the issues he explores are better addressed through an analysis of the discourse of the artistic community. He cites four main areas of difficulty with the practice of hip-hop transcription:

> ... the necessary level of specifity of a transcription, the ethical implications within the hip-hop community of transcribing a beat, the general values implicit in the close reading of a beat and the specific deficiencies of transcription as a mode of representation with regard to hip-hop. (Schloss, 2004, p. 13)

As part of his analysis of I. Emerge's World Series Turntable Championships routine, Katz notates a complex drum pattern, showing how a text and drum sample rhythmically fit together across 22 semiquavers (2005, p. 103). This is notated in a table using text to indicate the placement of samples used and numbers to indicate the semiquaver pulse.

Schloss finds a problem in the level of specifity needed for a transcription of the majority of the aesthetic elements he discusses, regarding them as either, 'too general, too specific, or too subjective' to benefit from a transcription-based analysis (2004, p. 13). Concerns are also raised regarding the ethical implications within the hip-hop community of transcribing beats. Publicly revealing the sources of particular samples is frowned upon and although techniques can be discussed, their realisation in specific cases cannot (ibid., p. 13). According to Middleton, however, the problems relating to the notation and transcription of popular music in general are diminishing as new forms of notation dealing with wider aspects of music are being developed (2000a, p. 5), necessitating new vocabularies and theoretical models for these uncharted areas, adding, '… it has become clear that how notation is used within the analytical method is more important than any inherent properties it may possess' (Middleton, 2000a, p. 5).

The last couple of decades have witnessed a significant development within turntable music, which, though not adopted by Schloss, may be useful in my analysis. As turntable techniques became more complex to execute and describe, members of the turntablist community began to acknowledge the need for a form of standardised notation to develop and exchange ideas within and outside the genre. Franklin Bruno (2001) regards this move to notation as inevitable owing to the expanding repertoire and its terminology. The numerous variables of pitch, volume, length and sound inherent in hip-hop turntable music have made this a challenging quest and the problems of notating a sound that is a synthesis of melody, harmony and rhythm has resulted in the existence of various techniques for notation and transcription. A number of approaches to notation have evolved to date, as practiced and developed by Radar (2000), Doc Rice (1998), Stephen Webber (2000), Carluccio, Imboden and Pirtle (2000), A-Trak (2000) and the Masterfaders crew (2001). All these approaches fall into two main approaches – those that draw on classical staff notation (Radar, Doc Rice and Webber) and those that have created a more graphic approach (Carluccio, Imboden and Pirtle, A-Trak and the Masterfaders). The majority of these notations relate only to the transcription of scratch patterns, although Carluccio, Imboden and Pirtle also offer a notation for other turntable techniques. The differences between these forms of notation lie not only in the choice of notation system, but also the reasons for their development.

Staff Notation

Radar

The notation developed by Radar relates primarily to scratch techniques and is an extension of the classical staff system of notation, Radar commenting, 'I'm not creating anything new, I'm merely adapting the turntables to the scoring of instruments known within the "western standard of music"' (Bruno, 2001). Radar's turntable composition, *Anti Matter*, is notated using the traditional method of bar lines and note and rest values and includes dynamic markings and articulation. Different instrumental elements of the composition, such as kick and snare drums, hi-hat, bass, vocals and even the scratch solo are notated on different staves, similar to traditional orchestration.

One major difference between traditional instrument notation and Radar's scratch notation however, is that Radar (a trained percussionist) omits any information relating to pitch. He commented on this decision at Skratchcon 2000, San Francisco, the world's first forum for the musical understanding of scratching and beat juggling:

> It's based on percussion ... you'd be able to do pitches with turntables, obviously, but with notation from a classical standpoint it's nearly impossible because you can't play chords on a turntable – you can play notes but you can't play chords. So I limit it to percussion and my score is based on percussion. (Radar 2000)

Radar includes information regarding articulation in his notation and in his lecture to Skratchcon 2000, he detailed the four basic articulations he has developed for use in his notation:

+ A forward cue (the performer pushes the record faster than the speed of the turntable).
- A drag cue (the performer pushes the record slower than the speed of the turntable).
= A back cue (the performer brings the record back).
O No cue (the hand is off the record, the turntablist manipulating the record using just the fader).

He cites one of the major reasons for his development of scratch notation as providing a communication link between turntablists and the general music community, controversially introducing staff notation at Skratchcon 2000 by saying that, 'this is music and this is how it's done ...' (Radar, 2000). He went on to describe how the use of more classical-based notational system would enable turntablism to be understood by classically trained musicians, opening up creative opportunities:

> I needed a system to talk to my colleagues and composers that work with ... I explain scratching to them and they don't understand it, but now they do and I am able to perform with great musicians ... great string players, great flautists, great piano virtuosos ... (Radar, 2000)

For Radar, this notational system offers a more traditional musical experience, giving the genre a rigorous theoretical foundation. Notation enables musicians to sight-read, a skill regarded by Radar as the cornerstone to the mastery of any musical instrument.

The need for the development of communication links with colleagues, composers and classical musicians gave rise to the second reason for Radar's development of scratch notation – legitimisation. Radar believes that the provision of a written and universal medium such as a score will establish turntablism as a legitimate form of musical expression and demonstrate to the wider musical community how the turntable can share a place in music history with the more established instruments. As Joseph Schloss comments, 'Notation is the language of the privileged art music, and people who want to be taken seriously in that world speak that language' (in Wang, 2000). Radar's traditional staff-based notation offers turntable musicians the opportunity to showcase and develop the turntable through a written universal medium that will provide a written history rather than one that is solely recorded. For Radar this legitimacy exists on two levels; firstly to establish turntablists as credible musicians and secondly to present turntablism as a true form of music requiring separate classification from other musical genres.

The third reason cited by Radar for the development of his scratch notation it that it demonstrates that turntable music is not necessarily based solely on improvisation (Kogun, 2001). The existence of a notational system and the possibilities of scores provide turntablists, and the wider musical community as a whole, with a new perspective to turntable techniques. It offers the musicians the opportunity to document their techniques and the composition as a whole, which, without notation, would have relied on memory:

> ... if we just go back and learn how to write for this instrument, we can take it to a higher level. That's what composition does, it takes it to a whole different level, because your brain can only remember so much. The thing is, when you write musical notation, it frees your mind, and it allows you to improve even more. (Ratz, 2001)

Doc Rice

In 1998, Doc Rice presented his third draft submission concerning the development of a viable notation method for turntable music. Rice adapts staff notation to accommodate turntable-specific features such as record movement and fader movement. Symbols are added onto the tails of standard note-symbols and define fader movement, which he divides into the three categories of freehand ('any scratch movement requiring no fader involvement'), strokes ('any scratch movements which can be categorized as starting with the sound in the off position, turned on momentarily') and clicks ('any scratch movements which can be categorized as starting with the sound in the on position, turned off momentarily').

Table 8.1   Doc Rice's three categories of fader movement

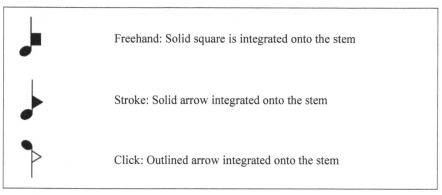

Freehand: Solid square is integrated onto the stem

Stroke: Solid arrow integrated onto the stem

Click: Outlined arrow integrated onto the stem

Source: Courtesy of Kimi 'Doc Rice' Ushida.

Doc Rice also created notation to indicate the directional movement of the record:

Table 8.2   Doc Rice's notation for the directional movement of the record

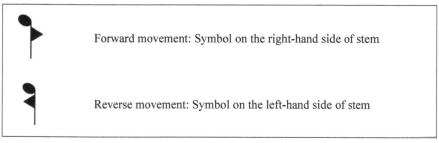

Forward movement: Symbol on the right-hand side of stem

Reverse movement: Symbol on the left-hand side of stem

Source: Courtesy of Kimi 'Doc Rice' Ushida.

These notations allow for both record and fader movements to be indicated on the staff. Unlike Radar, Rice addresses the aspect of pitch and the complications of working within a genre where pitch is relative, discussing the need for turntablists to relearn techniques which focus on speed and pitch combinations.

In a similar way to Radar, Rice's proposal was conceived from a 'traditional perspective' in order to allow for the interpretation and reproduction of turntable music by non-turntablist musicians (Rice, 1998). He writes that the notation will 'allow common ground between the conventional system and the new proposed system and will therefore incorporate as many similarities as possible' (Rice, 1998). However, he also recognises that to fully adopt staff notation, turntablism must tackle related aspects of the standard music system such as timing and pitch. Rice reflects that before any notational system can be developed, turntablists need to address how the genre should be interpreted by artists – whether as a new way to perceive music in the 'pattern-orientated style' implemented today and practiced without the boundaries of notes and scales, or in the traditional music systems of notes, pitches and time measures. Rice acknowledges that the choice of notation relates directly to the way in which turntablists and other musicians regard the genre.

Stephen Webber

For his book *Turntable Technique* (2000), which teaches the basics of scratching, Webber has developed a form of notation once more based on staff notation. The book gives beginners the option to develop their techniques whilst simultaneously learning the vocabulary of the 'universal language of music' (Webber, 2000). Webber comments that although reading staff notation is not a pre-requisite for being a turntablist musician, it offers the possibility for communication with other musicians. Reflecting the approach taken by both Radar and Doc Rice, Webber adapts traditional staff notation to incorporate elements specific to turntablism. Notes that represent the movement of the record are written below the staff, and arrows to show the direction of the turntable hand are written below these notes (Figure 8.1). Fader movements are written above the staff (Figure 8.2). The length of each note is determined by how long the fader stays up and so each note represents one of two moves; the fader being turned up (the attack of the note) and the fader being turned down (the release of the note). Like Radar, Webber also retains traditional notation for dynamics and incorporates articulation symbols including staccato, legato, short accents and long accents (Figure 8.3). All this information is notated on one staff (Figure 8.4).

Figure 8.1   Webber's notation for the movement of the record
and the direction of the hand on the turntable

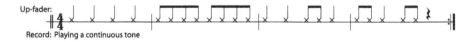

Figure 8.2   Webber's notation for fader movement

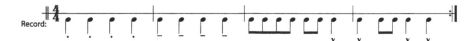

Figure 8.3   Webber's notation for articulation

Figure 8.4   Webber's staff
Source: Figures 8.1–8.4 courtesy of Stephen Webber and Berklee Press.

Graphic Notation

The earliest example of a graphical approach to turntable transcription was suggested as early as 1927 by H.H. Stuckenschmidt:

> ... the lines could be divided into definite rubrics and a fixed scheme established embracing all shades of tone-color, pitch and dynamic intensity. With this new script definite sounds could be transcribed. Sound waves would be shown in highly magnified form; in order to be transferred to the record they would need to be reduced by a photo-mechanical process. (Stuckenschmidt, cited in Katz, 2005, p. 107)

Such notation is not a record of the composition, but makes the composition itself, as the notation is made on the record itself, creating the sound (Katz, 107). More recent graphic approaches to turntable notation were developed and practiced by Carluccio, Imboden and Pirtle, A-Trak and The Masterfaders Crew.

Carluccio, Imboden and Pirtle

The TTM system (Turntable Transcription Methodology) developed by Carluccio, Imboden and Pirtle uses a method of angular lines representing the rotation and distance of travel of the record along the main 'staff' (Figure 8.5). The line slopes upward during the forward movement of the record and downward during the reverse movement (Figure 8.6). The sample being manipulated is noted at the side of the staff and the beat is highlighted so the speed of the sample can be ascertained. Running alongside more complex transcriptions is a second staff, indicating the positions of both the channel and cross-faders of the mixer, synchronised with the primary staff. A third staff underneath can be used in the event that the actions of a second turntable need to be recorded.

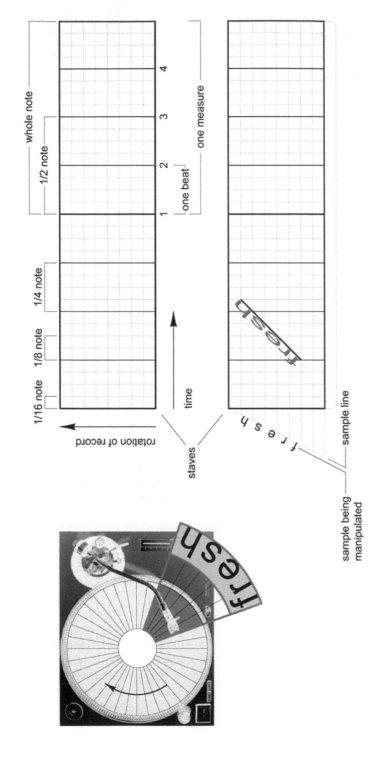

Figure 8.5   Carluccio, Imboden and Pirtle's notation for the rotation and distance of travel of the record
Source: Image courtesy of John Carluccio.

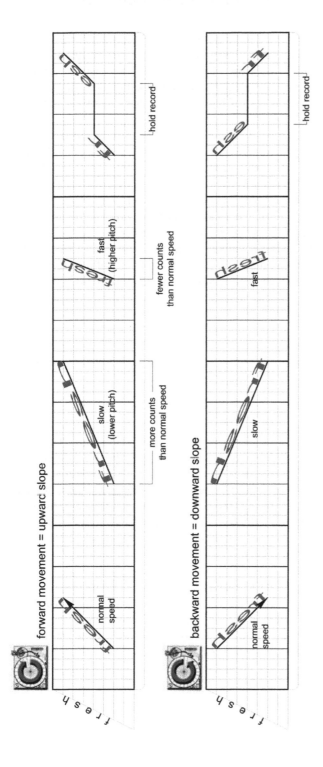

Figure 8.6   Carluccio, Imboden and Pirtle's notation for the movement of the record
Source: Image courtesy of John Carluccio.

Although this form of graphic notation gives time information through the placement of the sample on the graph, it provides no information regarding tempo. Carluccio, Imboden and Pirtle develop their notation for a variety of turntable techniques. As well as basic and advanced scratch notation, the transcription method offers visual representations of backspinning, drum symbols, delaying, chasing and tones, echoes and effects.

The Turntable Transcription Methodology (TTM) as developed by film director John Carluccio is a much more organic approach to notation than Radar's more ideological approach, and arose through a practical need to notate. Whilst filming a turntablist team he found himself struggling to describe an idea for a routine and so proceeded to scribble down different line patterns to convey his idea. In the TTM handbook (2001) the creators outline numerous reasons for its development. Firstly, TTM provides new perspectives. Structures are revealed and can be analysed and new structures emerge from this expanded understanding. This expansion of understanding may lead to the development of new techniques and patterns. Secondly, TTM acts as a creative tool, assisting individual artists in their musical development, enhancing the level of orchestration and musical design. Thirdly, communication facilitates progress and TTM gives the benefits of a language to a culture that currently only has an aural tradition. Techniques and routines can now be communicated anywhere. Finally, TTM supports the appreciation of turntablism, providing a method for documenting progress and preserving accomplishments.

A-Trak

A-Trak, like Carluccio, Imboden and Pirtle, places his notation in a graph. The x-axis represents the regular forward motion of a record over time, the y-axis represents the stretch of the record to be scratched. On this 'staff', each record movement is depicted as an angled line, with a positive or negative slope representing either a push forwards or a drag backwards respectively. In both Carluccio, Imboden and Pirtle's and A-Trak's notation, the speed and distance covered by each record manipulation is conveyed by the marks' height and steepness, therefore conveying information of pitch also:

> This translates to the angle of the line that I draw – if it's a high pitched scratch then it's a push on the record so there is a difference … a significant record movement over a small period of time … the line is at an important angle whereas if it's a low pitched scratch you're barely moving the record so the line will be at a much smaller angle. (A-Trak, 2000)

However, these lines are approximations more than detailed instructions, as A-Trak explains:

In general, everything is relative to what's around it. If you see that most of the scratches reach a certain height and then you have one that goes further vertically, you know that's a scratch that covers more of the record. (Bruno, 2001)

A-Trak's notation makes a direct link between the section of the record that is to be covered and the sound of the scratch. If the DJ barely moves the record back and forth on a very small section of the record you would hear a low-pitched scratch, but if the same movement in the same rhythm covered a larger section of the record a higher pitched scratch would be heard. He feels that there is little point in notating exact pitches unless the pitch of the sound source is known:

It would be irrelevant to get into more details with pitch. When you get on the table, the first scratch you do won't be exactly the pitch you want, and you have to play around with it until you get it. (Bruno, 2001)

Like Radar, A-Trak also utilises symbols to explain fader movements. However, A-Trak explains that he only uses symbols to avoid confusion adding, 'I don't think we should learn how to read a notation system, I think we should be able to look at it and visualise and understand what it is' (A-Trak, 2000). A crab scratch, for example, differs from a one-click orbit, not in the movement of the record, but in the manipulation of the fader. Radar's notation for this is a group of thirty-second note triplets, but A-Trak writes the simpler pattern with the picture of a crab.

Like Carluccio, Imboden and Pirtle's system, A-Trak's experiments into a notational system for scratching arose from a practical need, though where Carluccio, Imboden and Pirtle's need was documentation for documentation's sake, A-Trak notated to assist both his performance and compositional skills. Prior to some recording sessions where time would be limited, he would prepare his solos sometimes a day or two in advance:

... I was like, how am I going to remember this exactly? What if I forget one of the scratches? So instinctively, I just drew my scratches on a bit of paper the way I happened to see them in my head ... I drew them down and this way I got to the studio and looked at my sheet and remembered exactly which scratches to do and it was only later on when I thought back and realised that I was on to something with this whole notation thing. (A-Trak, 2000)

He acknowledges the impact this notation could have on this composition practice, through the increased potential for organisation and orchestration that notation offers. A-Trak's notation system also enables him to keep more detailed information about the style of the scratches. Writing the name of the scratch combinations rather than drawing them, he feels, would give no way of notating the length of the scratches or their exact placement within the music. He recognises that his system offers an easy way to visualise quite complex scratches, as the movement of the record, the use of the fader and the way these elements fit together are all visible.

Although A-Trak regards communication between DJs as a benefit of his notation system, he regards this as an additional benefit rather than a guiding force, commenting that whilst it's good for one DJ to be able to explain a scratch to another, notation should not become the standard method for turntablists to learn and communicate their craft:

> I'm not trying to impose this on anybody. If people don't believe in using notation, then they won't use it. But if someone's actually willing to find a use for it in their DJing, the same way that I have used for it in my world, then it's there. (Bruno, 2001)

However, during his lecture demonstration at Skratchcon 2000, he comments that his notation system would be extremely useful for those musicians who, while not being technically proficient, could envisage new patterns and scratches, adding a whole new dimension to constructing and orchestrating turntablist music.

The Masterfaders Crew

Like the notation developed by both Carluccio, Imboden and Pirtle and A-Trak, The Masterfaders Crew created a scratch notation that is graph-based. The relatively simple notation system uses a position versus time graph to follow the position of the turntablist's hand on the record, the x-axis representing time and the y-axis representing the position of the sample. The higher the point on the graph, the further the turntablist is into the sample and the lower the point on the graph, the closer they are to the beginning of the sample. If the line falls below the x-axis, it represents the turntablist moving the record to a point before the sample begins. Fader movement is represented by breaks in the line – discontinuities in the graph depict the fader in the off position, for example the notation of the 'stab' scratch technique. Very short discontinuities depict a quick fader click, for example the notation for the 'click' scratch technique. Time is represented by dark blue and light blue vertical lines, illustrating downbeats and up-beats respectively.

The Functions of Turntable Notation

Although the two main schools of notation are very different in approach, they both make possible the transcription and reproduction of previously undocumented techniques and patterns, between them highlighting five main functions of turntable notation:

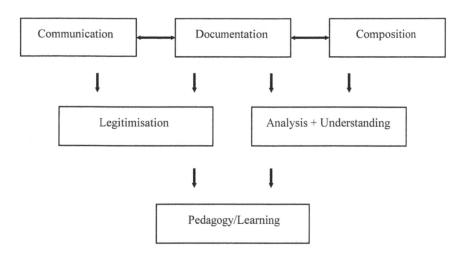

Figure 8.7   The five main functions of hip-hop turntable notation

What is evident is that the two schools, whilst having functions in common, display contrasting relationships between notation and composition. Whereas A-Trak sees notation as a compositional tool, for Radar, notation and composition are synonymous.

Radar's composition *Antimatter* was a technical exercise to demonstrate the feasibility of a fully notated turntable composition and the genre's legitimisation. Highly influenced by his classical training, Radar's use of traditional staff notation to both facilitate communication with classical musicians and to legitimise the genre via a written medium has led to the creation of a turntablist composition that was notated in its entirety prior to performance. This view of composition as a written discipline in its most rigid and traditional sense reflects Radar's desire for the creation of turntablist scores that can be learnt and performed by other turntablists. Radar regards *Antimatter* as a composition that '... represents the beginning of a new "Classical Era"' (Kogun, 2001), commenting, 'I think we are the future of music ... the turntablist of today is the Mozart of tomorrow' (Radar, 2000). This imposition of a classical system on to a relatively new genre in order to encourage and highlight legitimacy is not in keeping with the genre as a whole. As Schloss points out:

> ... as far as using Western notation, that's just ridiculous. That notation was created to represent the aesthetic values of a musical form that is very different from hip-hop. You basically end up arguing that Mozart would have dug turntablism. My question is, who cares? (Wang, 2000)

The shortcomings of Radar's notational approach for my analysis are two-fold. Not only does it disregard the compositional practices used by the majority of turntablist musicians in their assimilation of practice and composition, but it also necessitates the learning of relatively complex music theory, alienating non-classically trained musicians on both counts. Radar sends the message that the legitimisation of turntablism can only come via the classical music tradition. He implies that turntablism is on the wrong path, commenting that turntablists need to, '... go back and learn how to write for the instrument' (Ratz, 2001). Interestingly, it is A-Trak, with no institutional music training or prior knowledge of twentieth-century notation, who, unfettered by a search for legitimacy, has naturally chosen a more graphic and visual approach. A -Trak's notation system is used as a tool to aid composition rather than a system to compose in and seems to have developed naturally from within the genre in answer to an identified need in the compositional process. Both his system and TTM can be used to aid memory and pattern development during the process of composition, requiring no prior musical training, and so are immediately accessible to the majority of musicians working within the genre. Scratch pioneer Q-Bert reflects:

> Radar's notation is a little too complicated for me – you'd need to take up music I guess. The TTM is more the way I see it, and the way I'd try to notate it as well. (Wang, 2000)

The creators of TTM also acknowledge that the continual development of their notational system must be central to its success as it must absorb and reflect influences from within the genre rather than imposing an alien system onto the turntablist community. As Bruno comments, turntablism is currently in an awkward adolescence and the premature adoption of a given notation could stifle creativity. Turntablism deserves a notation that grows from its compositional practice, not one that dictates it.

A Notational System for the Analysis of Hip-Hop Team Turntable Compositions

The existing turntable transcription techniques are adequate when notating either for purposes of documentation or communication between musicians. However, any one of the approaches alone is not sufficient to fulfil the aims of an analysis of team turntable composition and therefore a new transcription method based on aspects of the existing systems has been developed. This method aims to encompass material, manipulation techniques and structure as well as tempo, timescale and the roles of individual musicians.

In developing this system of transcription, the notational approach developed by Radar has been rejected. The reasons for this are both practical and ideological. Radar's notation, like Webber's, is restricted to the transcription of scratch techniques and details only four basic articulations; a forward cue, a drag cue, a back cue and no cue. In doing so, it does not offer the visual representation of other important techniques such as backspinning or juggling that needs to be depicted. Rather than demonstrating the ways in which the records have been manipulated to achieve the sounds, Radar shows only how the rhythmic sounds are heard and for the purposes of this analysis, a notation is needed that allows the analysis of the techniques used by team members in the overall composition. He notates the different instrumental elements of the composition on different staves in the style of traditional staff notation, which Schloss (2004) regards as a shortcoming of much hip-hop notation, citing it as one of the main reasons for his rejection of transcription as a whole. Schloss comments that to present the sound as individual instrumental parts misrepresents the processes of sample choice and sound manipulation techniques, where sounds that may be heard as independent are often played from a single sample that consists of more than one instrument (2004, p. 14). The unsuitability of Radar's notation also lies in the different ideologies behind his technique and the analytical aims of this book. His notation has been developed to facilitate communication between musicians partly in order to legitimise the genre through a firm theoretical foundation. By pioneering the use of notation as a compositional technique in order to create a score that can be learnt and performed by other turntable musicians, Radar attempts to establish a written history for the genre. My notation, on the other hand, is purely for analytical purposes and though it could be used for compositional or communication purposes this was not the driving force behind its development.

Carluccio, Imboden and Pirtle, A-Trak and The Masterfaders Crew offer more useful approaches to hip-hop turntable notation as they offer graph-based depictions of specific sound manipulation techniques rather than, as Radar, only depicting the resulting sound patterns. By using these approaches it is possible to see how the records are used creatively, an important factor in my own analysis. However, it is Carluccio, Imboden and Pirtle who offer the fullest methodology, developing graphic representations of a range of techniques and so it will be mostly on his Turntable Transcription Methodology that this notation will be based, especially in the graphic depiction of sound creation and the adaptation of his score. To these elements have been added the colour-coding system to highlight the original material and types of sound manipulation used.

The top of the score gives information concerning the composers, name of composition, time signature and tempo. Each performer or turntable is designated a staff upon which their part is notated depending upon which remains most consistent during the performance. In the notation of the Scratch Perverts and the DMU Crew, for example, team members spent the majority of the time at one or two specific turntables so it was sensible to assign staves to individual artists. However, in the notation of the Mixologists, the two team members constantly moved turntables, making it more straightforward to assign a staff to each turntable that remained consistent throughout the performance.

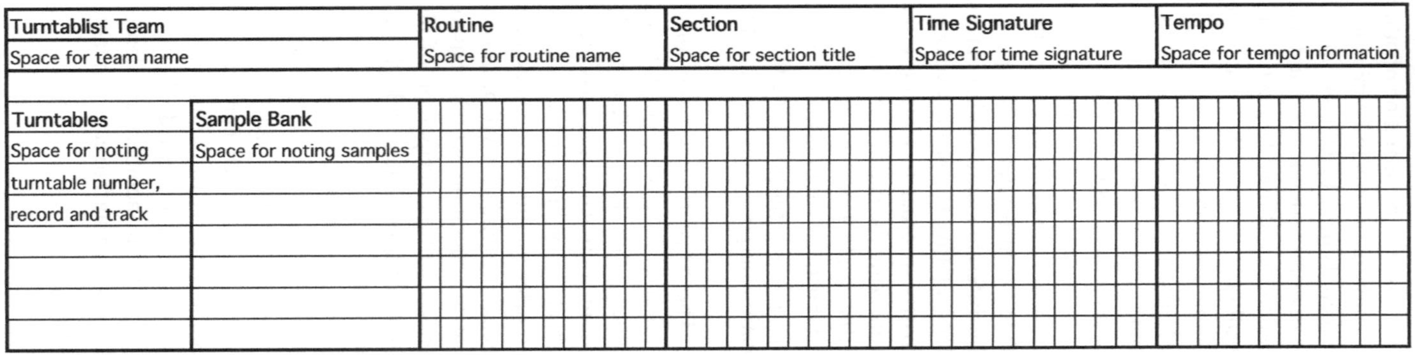

Turntablist Team	Routine	Section	Time Signature	Tempo
Space for team name	Space for routine name	Space for section title	Space for time signature	Space for tempo information

Turntables	Sample Bank
Space for noting turntable number, record and track	Space for noting samples

Figure 8.8   A score for the notation of hip-hop turntable routines

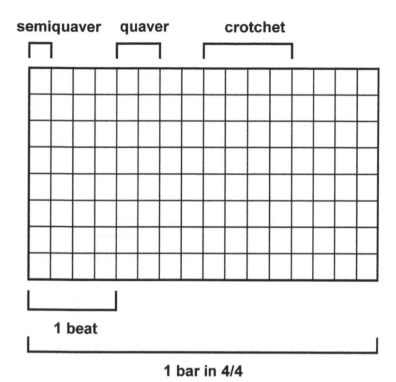

Figure 8.9   The staff, subdivided into bars and beats

The stave is derived from a graph of the rotation of the record versus time and runs from left to right. The vertical axis of the staff represents the rotation of the record and the horizontal axis represents time, subdivided into bars and beats (Figure 8.9). The basic staff is in 4/4 time, reflecting the usual time signature of the compositions to be analysed. Where the time signature alters, the change of time is written on the staff and the length of the bar is adjusted accordingly. Each stave has an area added to its left, the 'sample bank', to provide room for noting the record and track from which the samples to be manipulated originate, including colour coding to highlight the specific type of material used. This allows multiple samples at different locations on the record to be referenced in the score. Samples are written and numbered in the order that they appear during the composition and are colour coded according to the type of material; vocal samples are highlighted in pale yellow, melodic riffs and tones are highlighted in orange, drum-based material is highlighted in pale blue, atmospheric material is highlighted in dark blue and sound effects are highlighted in pale green. The numbers are then used on the stave to indicate a change in the sample being manipulated, though I shall also opt to write the sample next to the notation for ease of use during analysis. As, at times, there will not be enough room to write all of the sample information on the staff, tables including this information will be presented with the notation (volume two).

As in The Masterfaders' notation, a sample is drawn as a diagonal line on the staff, beginning when the sound starts and continuing to the point in the bar or phrase that the sound ends, taken from the Masterfaders' notation (Figure 8.10). The higher the point on the graph, the further the turntablist is into the sample, and the lower the point on the graph, the closer s/he is to the beginning. The horizontal distance is therefore determined by the amount of time it takes to play the sample. When a record is played forwards, the line has an upward slope; when it is played backwards it has a downwards slope.

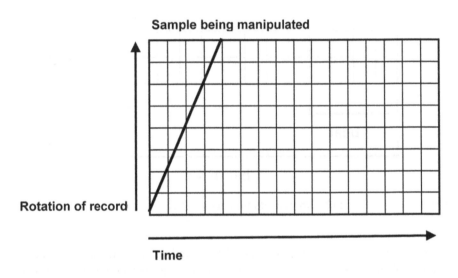

Figure 8.10   The rotation of the record versus time

The different sound manipulation techniques used by the musicians are depicted on the staff and a number of techniques not transcribed in Carluccio, Imboden and Pirtle's method have been included, including beat juggling, looping with stickers and using the audio signal cable as a sound source. To assist the analysis and for overall clarity these techniques have been colour-coded to increase their visibility. The techniques have been placed into seven categories:

Table 8.3   The depiction of sound manipulation techniques

Technique	Explanation	Colour/symbol
Punchphasing	A section of the record being played either solo or alongside samples performed on other turntables.	Blue
Backspinning	The record being spun back to locate a sample to be repeated. This can either be audible or muted by the fader movement.	Aqua marine
Use of the pitch regulator	The musician using the pitch regulator to achieve melodic effects.	Lilac
Rhythm from an audio signal cable	The use of the finger tapping a connected cable to create additional rhythms. Where this is used, the rhythm is also depicted by placing a black square in the beats where the sound is heard.	Dark orange
Scratching	Different scratching techniques are used.	Pink
Beat Juggling	The technique of one musician using a pair of records playing the same sample across two turntables.	Green
Tapping	The musician tapping the record to create a rhythmic effect.	Pale orange
Record left to run	A section of the record is left to play, free from any manipulation.	Grey

The different types of sample material have also been categorised:

Table 8.4   Depiction of sample material

Type of sample	Colour code
Vocals	Pale yellow
Melodic riffs and tones	Orange
Drums	Pale blue
Atmospheric pads	Dark blue
Sound effects	Pale green

On the main body of the score a striped colour method has been used, alternating the colour coding for the sample material and technique used. This allows the reader to see these two elements simultaneously.

Symbols also appear in the score to represent other occurrences such as changing the record, hand clapping, the use of sticker loops, the generation of a tone from an audio signal cable and the continuation of the record from one page to the next.

Table 8.5   The depiction of other occurrences

Other occurrences	Symbol
Changing the record	
Hand-clapping	
Tone from audio cable	
Sticker loops	
Record continues from previous page	
Record continues to next page	

Rather than over-complicating a reading of the score through a profusion of symbols, comments can also be written on the score, which are quicker to process for analytical purposes.

The representation of the composition in this way allows a comparison of the structural techniques used by the composers from section to section of the composition, thus tracking repetition, development and possible patterns of creation a well as to log the specifics of the sound manipulation techniques being carried out. Through using the score, it is possible to establish the structure of the composition in relation to sound generation and sound manipulation techniques as well as tempo and timescale and the roles of individual musicians within the composition. The ability to isolate sonic and rhythmic patterns and their development throughout the work makes it possible to establish in greater detail the way in which the turntable teams create the composition. This development of both a suitable framework and detailed notation for the study of turntable music enables a full discussion of the compositional processes of hip-hop turntable teams, specifically the work of the Scratch Perverts, the Mixologists and the DMU Crew. The full transcriptions of the three analysed routines are available to download from www.turntablecollaboration.com.

Chapter 9

Analysis of the Compositional Process of UK Hip-Hop Teams

This chapter will discuss and analyse one routine from each of the three teams discussed in this book, firstly that of the DMU Crew, then that of The Mixologists and finally that of the Scratch Perverts. The analysis will focus on what Farrell (2001) calls the stage of 'collective action', which to reflect the particular collaborative nature of turntable composition I have re-named 'collective creation'. Through the analysis, the collaborative processes and techniques used in the creation of team turntable routines will be explored, establishing any characteristics of hip-hop team turntable compositions, rather than focusing on a deep musicological analysis of the completed routines. To gain the best possible insight into such processes, the analysis of each routine will be split into two main parts. The first will discuss the process of collective creation in relation to the devising framework as established in Chapter 4, including pre-devising administration, preliminary rehearsals, rehearsals phase one and two and final rehearsals and performance. At the beginning of the discussion concerning each of the five stages, the main elements will be bullet-pointed, as established in the model framework. The second will analyse the completed routine through the analytical framework established in Chapter 5, discussing the timing, group organisation, general properties, sample choice, sound manipulation techniques, structure and texture of the routine as a whole. Following the analysis of both the creative process and the resulting artistic product, a number of characteristics of team turntable composition will be established, based on the findings from the three routines. In the case of each routine, the individual sections were not named by the teams but have been named to aid the analysis.

DMU Crew Routine, Leicester May 2002

1. Context

This routine was created by the Leicester-based turntable team the DMU Crew for performance in Leicester in May 2002. Data for the analysis of the process of collective creation was collected through non-participant observation and formal interviewing. The four member Leicester-based team was videoed over a period of six rehearsals in which they created and developed a turntable routine for performance. The formal interview took place after the rehearsal process, and was recorded on tape. The analysis of the completed routine was made using video footage of the final rehearsal of the routine and so the accompanying documentary evidence from which the notation and analysis was taken contains some extraneous talking which is not relevant to the routine. Although footage of the performance exists, the sound quality is inferior to that of the rehearsal and so has not been used for analysis. The individual sections of the routine have not been named by the team, but have been given titles by myself to aid analysis of the whole composition. For purposes of anonymity, the four team members will be referred to as Member 1, Member 2, Member 3 and Member 4.

2. The Process of Collective Creation

Stage One: Pre-devising Administration

- Team building
- Establish the working parameters of the group
- Allocation of roles
- Establish skills of individuals
- Establish common artistic ground

In the creation of the DMU Crew's routine, much of the pre-devising administration occurred before rehearsals, both socially and in alternative creative contexts. Individual group members were known to each other before, having either worked together or lived together previously. This meant that both social and creative work parameters had already been formed and common artistic ground had been established prior to the rehearsal process. At this early stage of the creative process, roles were assigned according to the strengths and weaknesses of each group member. Member 2 explains in interview how, as the most competent at various scratch techniques, he was given the role as scratch musician and as Member 1 and Member 3 were the most competent beat matchers, this role was assigned to them. Member 4, as the lowest skilled group member, was given the role of punching sounds over the top of the main body of the composition and also creating atmospheric textures by using loops of sound (DMU Crew, 2003). Roles also developed to reflect non-musical skills. Member 1, for example, took a more directorial role, commenting that he naturally 'dominates any situation' (DMU Crew, 2003). When interviewed, Member 2 and Member 1 both communicated that they felt that their roles were more directorial than the other group members, though added that this was partly due to practical reasons. The rehearsal studio was set up at their home and therefore they had more access and time to work on the performance outside designated rehearsal times than other group members. Member 1 added, '[We] spoke about it a lot ... we worked out probably the best plan between us and then told the others about it and discussed it with them' (DMU Crew, 2003).

Stage Two: Preliminary Rehearsals

- Discuss theme and end product
- Establish parameters for a constructive process
- Generate and share ideas
- Create and share material

The first and second rehearsals of the DMU Crew could be seen as preliminary rehearsals. From the transcription of the first rehearsal, it is evident that the theme and end product of the artistic work were discussed early on in the process. Within the first half of the rehearsal, team members discussed what they felt the end product should be. In interview, Member 1 explained how, prior to the rehearsal process, he had thought that the group might have found it difficult to decide and agree on a theme and product, whereas in reality, they managed to agree fairly quickly (DMU Crew, 2003). Establishing aims for the artistic work was especially important and would help in both the initial idea stage and the later development of the work:

> We had to look at the aims of what we had to do and we also knew what we wanted to incorporate in there as much as possible ... we had a time it had to last for and we worked around that. (Member 1, in DMU Crew, 2003)

For Member 1, this was a natural process as it enabled him to approach the process and performance in the same way that he would any creative project, by establishing the audience, their reasons for attending the performance and the performative context and then creating an artistic product and performance that would suit such criteria (DMU Crew, 2003).

Much of the first rehearsal was spent generating and sharing ideas. The group was extremely excited about working together across four turntables and they began experimenting with material and combinations of material almost immediately. Specific material to be found and developed was discussed, including a long tone or pad sound to be developed into a melodic line through utilization of the turntables' pitch control and platter speed. Ideas for other sections of the piece were shared and discussed, including an idea for a 'clap your hands' section and the location of the material needed for it. Group members worked within their allocated roles. Member 1 experimented with beat matching, cross fading and backspinning, experimenting with the different effects that can be achieved with the mixer faders. He also continuously changed the records to try different combinations of sound, cutting different tracks in and out. Member 2 experimented with scratch patterns, both instrumental and vocal, trying different styles and techniques as well as backspinning. The group members shared the same technical set-up and so were creating music together from the outset, though at times they worked independently from each other.

The second rehearsal was entirely spent generating and sharing material and ideas, team members working simultaneously on the equipment. Member 1 and Member 3 mixed and beat-matched using three turntables between them, Member 2 scratching on the remaining deck. Once more, Member 1 and Member 3 constantly changed records, both independently and simultaneously, experimenting with different style changes and textures, for example using the fader to punch small bursts of one record over another or using the faders of two mixers simultaneously to mix between records. As well as experimenting individually, group members also worked together. At times, for example, Member 1 and Member 3 shared a turntable and a mixer, Member 1 manipulating the fader whilst Member 3 used the turntable. No member of the group was restricted to a particular turntable but was able to move freely between decks, at one point resulting in Member 2 scratching with the line switch to allow Member 3 to use the fader to bring in a record. Member 2, reflecting his role as scratch specialist, experimented with different scratch patterns and scratching on different places on the record as well as scratching vocal samples. However, he was not restricted by his role and did experiment with some beat matching. Different roles came to the fore throughout the rehearsal, the group working together to experiment with different styles, textures and structures.

Stage Three: Phase 1 Rehearsals

* Establish structure and creative framework
* Create basic 'template'
* Generate material
* Try sections

Phase one of the rehearsal process outlined in the model framework of the devising process is evident in the third rehearsal for the turntable team. It is apparent that during this rehearsal much more focus was placed on structure, order and content than in earlier rehearsals. In the first 15 minutes of the rehearsal, Member 1 and Member 2 discussed the opening structure of the developing composition and Member 1 outlined his views on the performance being structured in two parts. The first of these he identified as a '... soundscapey blend of things ...' (DMU Crew, 2002) and the second a more rhythmically-based section. When interviewed, Member 1 and Member 2 described the importance of having a structure early in the process, deciding first on a framework and then working on what to put in it. Member 1 commented:

> I think we were constantly mindful of the structure ... the way I think is best to approach performances is to start at the end – work out what you want from the performance and then work your way backwards ... I think the structure of the performance is probably what you need to have first. (DMU Crew, 2003)

However, as is reflected in this third rehearsal, the creative process happens much more organically at times: structure and material developing simultaneously. Member 1 and Member 2 discussed ways in which the material they have already could be developed through structuring the piece differently (DMU Crew, 2002). In the interview Member 1 reflected:

> ... we were constantly thinking about what we'd end up doing or we were messing around with loads of ideas at the same time. And then we were fed up with messing around with loads of ideas ... [we'd think] we need to start to get something concrete. (DMU Crew, 2003)

In addition, a major factor in this first rehearsal stage of the devising process was the generation of material that in turn would be placed into the determined structure. Much of the third rehearsal was spent searching through records for the desired sounds or textures as well as experimenting with and discussing the sounds already found, a process made simpler by the group members' expert knowledge of their record collections:

> I know instantly there were a couple of my records – obviously I know my record collection pretty much inside out – so it didn't take too long to think of a number of options. (Member 1, DMU Crew, 2003)

The majority of material generated and discussed during this phase one rehearsal was for the opening sections. Early on in the rehearsal, Member 1 skill-shared with Member 4, directing him in the creation of material for the opening section, consisting of looped textures. This skill-sharing is also evident in Member 3's relationship with Member 1, when later in the rehearsal he is directed by Member 1 how to loop a section of record using stickers placed on the vinyl.

Looking for ways to generate material led the group members to develop new techniques, something that Member 1 regards as important for the performance (DMU Crew, 2002). One new approach for the group was to generate and develop more textural material (DMU Crew, 2003). Another new approach was demonstrated by Member 2 who experimented with stickers on the surface of the record as well as achieving different tones through manipulating the platter:

> ... the tape on the records was a new thing for us to do ... there was a lot of doing that actually, working out and timing up the loops and everything – that was quite good fun ... proper hands on. (Member 1, DMU Crew, 2003)

In turn, these new approaches affected the sections in which they were integrated. The clicking sound from records looped by stickers for example, could not be avoided and so an undesirable sound that would normally be avoided was made intentional and is indeed central to the section (DMU Crew, 2002).

As well as developing and generating material for the sections and transitions, the team members continually discussed the relevance of the material and its pertinence in the section in which it has been placed as well, as ways in which desired affects could be practically achieved. At this stage, the group tried out elements of the section to ascertain their suitability and success, but the sections were mostly planned out through discussion. During the rehearsal, Member 1 and Member 2 discussed the two sections at length, referring to the sounds, textures, Member 1ings and structure of the section as well as the need for a transition between the two. Member 1 commented:

> If we could get a neat perfect loop, something that hasn't got beats in it that is a perfect fit then we can gradually bring that in to the other clicky [material] and if we get one perfect loop ... we can use that as a metronome and start being more structured and make a transition towards a more rhythmic structural composition and gradually start mixing beats ... (DMU Crew, 2002)

Stage Four: Phase 2 Rehearsals

- Develop ideas and content
- Set and work on individual and group tasks
- Share with group
- Select and discard material
- Confirm content and clarify sections
- Reflect and evaluate
- Re-work according to feedback

Phase two of the process outlined in the model framework of the devising process is evident in the fourth and fifth of the group's rehearsals. A substantial amount of time during these rehearsals was spent by group members developing both ideas and content, often in relation to the developing structure. Member 1, Member 2 and Member 3 began the fourth rehearsal by experimenting with loops and textures and discussed how this material could be ordered structurally to improve the clarity of the section. Member 1 suggested:

> All of us ... just fading it in and out gently so that no-one really knows who's doing what when – there are just loads of different sounds coming from everywhere ... each person has got to do their own thing once or twice ... that's long enough ... (DMU Crew, 2002)

The members looked for specific material and experimented with it, through a variety of turntable techniques such as adjusting the speed or dragging the platter, to achieve new textures or a specific effect. Group members tried different approaches to the material and discussed their findings in depth. This development of material was often undertaken by individuals as well as by the group as a whole. In the second half of rehearsal four, for example, Member 1, Member 2 and Member 3 worked independently from each other for a short time, Member 1 making loops of material by placing stickers on the vinyl and Member 2 and Member 3 looking for specific material, discussing together the type of material they required (DMU Crew, 2002). In interview, Member 1 described how he and Member 2 also worked independently on the composition away from the designated rehearsals:

> ... it was a bit of a novelty having four decks and everything and you always want to have a bit of a mess about ... we tried some stuff [but] I don't think we were necessarily more creative than the others ... (DMU Crew, 2003)

Member 1 highlighted how all the group members developed ideas away from the main rehearsals, commenting that they would all come to rehearsals with new ideas (DMU Crew, 2003).

This sharing of ideas and material continued throughout rehearsals four and five, including the development of new techniques (such as using the feedback sound from a live audio cable as a sound source and running the record against the needle) as well as sharing suggestions about material and the way in which to use it. The material and ideas shared with other members were then discussed to ascertain the suitability for the composition. Member 1 and Member 2 explain in interview how all group members had an opportunity to input their ideas into the creative process. Once the ideas or material had been shared, the members chose to select, experiment with or discard the material. For the team, this did not appear to be a particularly negative experience, possibly due to the good relationship that existed between them. Member 1 reflected in interview that there was no friction between members commenting, 'we just spoke about things and worked out what we thought was good – but what we all thought was good.' (DMU Crew, 2003). Member 1 explained that decisions were only made when the group as a whole came to an agreement that the choice was the right one and that its incorporation would be beneficial to the composition:

> I think the only way to work if you're working with people is when you agree on something ... if all parties agree on something you know pretty much that you've got the right answer ... We all decided what we'd do together so everyone was comfortable with it. (DMU Crew, 2003)

He went on to describe how, in the early stages of the decision making process, some group members were slow to comment, a problem that he dealt with through his more directorial role:

> If you're thrashing an idea out between you, everyone has got different ideas – good points and bad points – about different things and might not necessarily really want to say so until someone sort of makes the first move ... so when you've got that element of doubt I tend to be that person who makes the first

move. I don't know whether that's guidance as such or putting the cat amongst the pigeons for the sake of thrashing out the answer. I tend to be fairly forward at speaking my mind so I don't know whether that had much influence over the process. (DMU Crew, 2003)

Ideas were also discarded if they were deemed as being too technically difficult. Member 2, for example, experimented with a new technique of placing a cartridge upside down underneath the record to play it backwards. The record sits a couple of inches above the platter and the cartridge fits underneath the record so instead of resting it on top of the record, the cartridge is lifted up onto the bottom of the vinyl. This idea was eventually discarded as it presented too many technical problems (DMU Crew, 2003).

The majority of time spent in phase two of the rehearsal process was taken up with confirming content and clarifying sections and the overall structure of the composition. Member 2 explains how the structure was built up from a number of sections that highlighted different turntable techniques. This was then developed further, in 'different ways with different kinds of sounds' (DMU Crew, 2003) with the input of group members. Member 1 added:

> We started off with textural bits and pieces ... and worked out if we had enough textural material and enough interesting stuff to do with that for the relevant period of time. When that was done, we went for the loop clicks and then ended up going for beatmatching stuff because by then we'd covered a few different techniques ... different from what we usually do ... We set it up in sections and ... thought it might be a little bit more interesting ... (DMU Crew, 2003)

The group members spent much of the fourth and fifth rehearsals confirming the content that would go into each of these sections. Lengthy and detailed discussions were had between group members, covering the roles and activities of the members during performance, cues, timings and details such as volume and panning. As well as the content of the main body of the composition and any transition sections, these discussions also covered different combinations of material and textures and how best to mix and blend them together. Every detail of content was picked over by the group and sometimes followed up with practical demonstrations, further experiments and attempts at piecing the sections together. This highly detailed analysis enabled the group to see if there were any areas that had not been fully considered or any other material that was needed. A large proportion of time during these rehearsals was spent clarifying sections, their place in the overall structure and the implications of this for the group members. Many discussions dealt with the order of the records, the best way for the sections to fit together and the intricacies and relationships between group members during the performance. Clarification of sections became increasingly complex when the group began to piece the sections together, mapping out the group members' use of records and turntables and taking into account which record was required by which artist on which turntable, bearing in mind that some artists shared material from the same record and members moved between turntables. Member 2 described how roles and responsibilities would be assigned to team members:

> … We said this bit is being done by this person … and this person needs to be doing something because they are not doing anything, so they can do that bit … (DMU Crew, 2003)

Member 1 added:

> We wanted to try and keep as many people active at the same time as possible. There was obviously the potential for it to be pretty boring – three people just stood there staring at the crowd and one person doing something for fifteen minutes – whether you're taking it in turns or not. (DMU Crew, 2003)

As is evident from the discussion and creative activities that took place throughout this second phase of rehearsals, reflection and evaluation occurred throughout the creative process of the group and was inextricably linked to other elements of the phase such as developing ideas and content, selecting and discarding material, sharing with the group, confirming content and clarifying sections. Indeed this whole phase can be seen to reflect the 'inner cycle of development and evaluation' as outlined by Landy and Jamieson and discussed earlier in this Chapter.

Phase 5: Final Rehearsals and Performance

- Rehearse and perform

Once they were happy with the routine, the DMU Crew set aside a specific period for rehearsal of the finished piece. They regarded this aspect of the creative process as vital for developing confidence prior to the performance, to ensure that all members were comfortable with their own parts and roles and responsibilities. This rehearsal period gave the performers the opportunity not only to be confident with their own parts, but also more aware of how these parts link with others and to practice the cues:

> … it's something that you develop while you're practising it, realising that those people are doing that while you're doing this, so you can remember for next time that you're at the right place with everyone else. (DMU Crew, 2003)

Although the majority of the time during this phase was spent rehearsing the routine, a small amount of time was also spent refining both material and structure. Members reflected on the sections throughout the rehearsals and discussed material, cues and transitions between sections whilst they performed (DMU Crew, 2002). Following the run-throughs of the routine the team discussed and evaluated particular aspects, including the material (for example, Member 4's rhythmic motif with the lead and how to end the routine), cues (for example, whether or not these should be audio or visual) and structure (for example, the length of sections and the routine as a whole) (DMU Crew, 2002).

3. Group Organisation

All group members perform in each of the sections. Positions do not change at all during the piece, members using the same equipment throughout. Member 4 uses turntable one, Member 1 uses turntable two and the pair share mixer one. Member 3 uses turntable three, Member 2 uses turntable four and the pair share mixer two. In the third section, 'Bass and Scratch' Member 4 does not perform using turntable one, instead performing using a lead connected to mixer one.

4. General Properties

The routine lasts for 11 minutes and 12 seconds. It consists of three sections, 'Texture', 'Click and Clap' and 'Bass and Scratch', which range from 2 minutes 48 seconds to 4 minutes 44 seconds in length.

Table 9.1   Duration of individual sections within the routine

	Texture	**Click and Clap**	**Bass and Scratch**	**Total**
Timing	4 mins 44 secs	2 mins 48 secs	3 mins 40 secs	11 mins 12 secs
Bar length	71 bars	88 bars	76 bars	235 bars

All sections are in 4/4 time. The tempos of the sections vary, the first being 58 beats per minute, the second 124 beats per minute and the third being 90 beats per minute. The soundscape quality of section one, 'Texture', means that there is little sense of pulse, but tempo and timescale have been imposed for analytical purposes.

Table 9.2   Time signature and tempo of individual sections

	Texture	**Click and Clap**	**Bass and Scratch**
Time signature	4/4	4/4	4/4
Tempo (Beats per minute)	58	124	90

5. Sample Choice

The composition uses 20 samples, six vocal, 12 instrumental and two textural. Their division across the individual sections is as follows:

Table 9.3   Sample types used in the routine

	Instrumental	Instrumental and vocal	Sound effect	Textural	Vocal
Texture	3	0	0	2	1
Click and Clap	4	0	0	0	1
Bass and Scratch	5	0	0	0	4

Instrumental samples
The instrumental samples are the largest category, making up 60 per cent of all samples used, and they fall into three instrumental types. The largest category is single tone samples, totalling seven, followed by three drum samples and two bass samples. The greatest use of instrumental samples is in the 'Click and Clap' section where 80 per cent of all samples used are instrumental. Instrumental samples are also the largest category in 'Texture', totalling 50 per cent and 'Bass and Scratch', totalling 56 per cent.

Vocal samples
Vocal samples are the second largest category used throughout the section, totalling 30 per cent of all samples used. All are spoken male voices. These samples increase in use throughout the composition, from 17 per cent in 'Texture', to 20 per cent in 'Click and Clap' and 44 per cent in 'Bass and Scratch'.

Atmospheric samples
These types of samples are used only by the DMU Crew and take the form of atmospheric samples with a soundscape quality. These types of samples are used only in the opening section, two making up 33 per cent of all samples used.

6. Structure

All sections in the routine are structured around the layering together of different samples and repeated patterns.

Texture
The 'Texture' section is not strictly structured, but relies on a pre-agreed framework built around sound cues. The section is loosely structured in three sections of 24

bars, each section seeing the introduction of a prominent sample that cues the rest of the team, allowing the section to develop.

Click and Clap

The structure of this section is again determined by the layering different of samples. The section cannot be divided into smaller sections as only three sample layers dominate (all of which are short one-bar phrases) to which drums and vocals are added later. Members enter one at a time, adding a new layer and after playing simultaneously, leave in turn.

Bass and Scratch

Once more, the section is structured around the gradual inclusion and exclusion of layers that overlap structurally to allow different combinations of parts. The opening and ending of the section are symmetrical and, in the middle, individual parts come and go in a succession of four bar phrases.

7. Sound Manipulation Techniques

The DMU Crew use five main sound manipulation techniques – mixing, punchphasing, backspinning, scratching and sticker looping.

Mixing

Both Member 1 and Member 3 use mixing techniques. Member 1 mixes in all of the sections and Member 3 mixes in the first and third sections. Both mix using textural samples and instrumental samples. Member 4 and Member 2 do not use mixing techniques.

Punchphasing

Punchphasing is used in all sections and is shared between three team members, Member 4, Member 2 and Member 3. Member 4 is the sole member to punchphase instrumental samples, using them only in the first section. Member 2 and Member 3 both punchphase vocal samples during the routine, Member 2 using the technique in all sections and Member 3 only using the technique in the final section.

Backspinning

Member 4 and Member 2 both use backspinning techniques. Member 4 is the only member to backspin instrumental samples and Member 2 is the only member to backspin vocal samples. The final section, 'Bass and Drum', contains no backspinning. Neither Member 3 nor Member 1 uses the technique.

Scratching

Member 2 and Member 3 both use scratching techniques. Member 2 scratches in each section using both instrumental samples and vocal samples. Member 3 also scratches vocal samples, but does so only in the final section. Member 1 and Member 4 do not use any scratching techniques.

Sticker loops
The sticker loop technique is used by Member 4, Member 3 and Member 2 but only in the 'Click and Clap' section. In this technique, a small sample repeats automatically as the needle hits a sticker placed at the end of the sample that makes it jump to the beginning of the sample again. Each sticker loop sample lasts for one bar and is repeated for as long as is required.

Audio signal cable
Although it is not a sound manipulation technique, Member 4 creates a rhythmic pattern using a lead connected to one of the mixers. He alone uses this technique.

As is apparent from the information above, some of the manipulation techniques are shared between members whilst only one group member takes others on. To look more closely at the roles of individual group members and the use of sound manipulation techniques within the routine as a whole I have developed a system of grading the sound manipulation techniques used by each member. In their uses of the techniques, each group member is either a primary user – a group member who uses the technique frequently; a secondary user – a group member who used the technique, but less frequently than the primary user; or a minimal user – a group member who uses the technique very infrequently.

Member 1 is a primary user of mixing techniques using both instrumental and textural samples. Member 4 is a primary user of punchphasing and backspinning instrumental samples. She is also a primary user of sticker-looping instrumental samples and audio signal cable rhythm techniques. Member 3 is a primary user of mixing techniques using textural samples and sticker looping techniques using instrumental samples. He is a secondary user of punchphasing and scratching techniques with vocal samples as well as mixing techniques with instrumental samples. Member 2 is a primary user of the punchphasing and backspinning techniques using vocal samples. He is a primary user of scratching techniques both of vocal and instrumental samples. He is also a primary user of sticker-looping techniques using instrumental samples. Some group members are the only individuals to use a particular technique. Member 4, for example, is the sole user of punchphasing and backspinning instrumental samples as well as using the audio signal cable. Member 2 is the sole user of backspinning techniques using vocal samples and scratching instrumental samples. Some group members are primary users of the same techniques and work together, for example Member 1 and Member 3 who both use mixing techniques to manipulate textural samples in the opening section and Member 4, Member 2 and Member 3 who share sticker looping techniques using instrumental samples to create the second section. Some group members support others' primary use of techniques with their secondary techniques. Only Member 3 is a secondary user, supporting Member 1 by mixing instrumental samples and Member 2 by scratching and punchphasing vocal samples.

Table 9.4   DMU Crew: Manipulation techniques and their users

	Member 1	Member 4	Member 3	Member 2
Punchphasing vocal samples			░	■
Punchphasing instrumental samples		■		
Punchphasing textural samples				
Backspinning vocal samples				■
Backspinning instrumental samples		■		
Backspinning textural samples				
Scratching vocal samples			▨	■
Scratching instrumental samples				
Scratching textural samples				
Mixing vocal samples				
Mixing instrumental samples	■		▨	
Mixing textural samples	■		■	
Sticker-looping vocal samples				
Sticker-looping instrumental samples		■	■	■
Sticker-looping textural samples				
Audio Signal Cable rhythmic pattern		■		

Key

Primary user of technique	■
Secondary user of technique	▨
Minimal use of technique	░

8. Texture

In all three sections, the predominance of layering means that the texture is built up gradually, each part entering and leaving in turn. There is a difference in texture between sections, however. The first section, 'Texture', is relatively dense, whereas 'Click and Clap' and 'Bass and Scratch' are lighter in texture. In the main, this is not due to the number of musicians performing in the different sections, as at least three play relatively consistently throughout. Instead, this variation is caused by the nature of samples that dominate in each section. In the opening section, the texture is created through the predominance of atmospheric samples that play continuously. These are layers of sound rather than individual vocal or instrumental samples. This ensures that even when only two musicians perform simultaneously the texture is still heavy. There is no melody line and the building of textures and the relationship between them is central. In both 'Click and Clap' and 'Bass and Scratch', however, the texture is lighter. Although musicians often perform simultaneously, the samples used are either instrumental or vocal and contain only one sound at a time, unlike the soundscape quality of the samples used in the opening section. In 'Bass and Scratch', this is intensified by fewer simultaneous performers. For the majority of the section only two members perform together and all four perform simultaneously for only two bars in total.

In the first two sections of the routine, no one part is predominant. All layers are equally important and the texture is created through the layering of these parts. In both sections, the texture remains quite static throughout but interest is created through the overlapping patterns of the different layers and the slight variation in texture that this creates. This is also because the samples used do not always loop in time with each other, which creates interesting patterns over time. In 'Bass and Scratch' however, the different combinations of layered parts change frequently, often every four bars, and so the texture is more varied.

The Mixologist Routine, London, September 2001

1. Context

This routine was created by the London-based turntable team The Mixologists – Beni G and Go. It was made for performance at the DMC 2001 World Team Championship (formally the DMC DJ Team Championship) at the London Apollo in September 2001, where the team competed against twelve other turntable teams from around the world. The information for the analysis of the creative process has been gathered through interviews with the Mixologist team in 2001 and 2002. The notation and analysis of this routine was taken from video footage of the performance published by the DMC (2001).

2. The Process of Collective Creation

Stage One: Pre-devising administration

- Team building
- Establish the working parameters of the group
- Allocation of roles
- Establish skills of individuals
- Establish common artistic ground

For The Mixologists, 'pre-devising' administration occurred prior to the creation of the routine. The two team members work together as professional DJs performing in clubs around the UK and this is the second routine that they created for the DMC team championship final. The individual skills of the members and the general allocation of roles were established before the creation of this routine, as were the working parameters of the group. The common artistic approach of team members is based on two premises, both of which are reflected in this routine. Firstly, a routine must incorporate different sorts of music and secondly, it has to offer something new. The most important impetus behind The Mixologists' creation of routines is that they must create something original, finding samples that have not been used before to create 'fresh' sounds:

> You'll always be thinking "Is this going to work well? Is it going to be too cheesy? Has someone already done it?" You're always thinking about that when you get samples, when you get sounds and get ideas. (Beni G, 2002)

Beni G feels that the 2001 routine reflected this approach, incorporating both new samples and recognisable samples used differently:

> … when I watched it, it was nice to know that all these different sounds and the sounds we were using, a lot of people had never used or heard before. Or they might have heard before, but they hadn't ever thought of using it in a battle routine and it wasn't the same old samples being chopped up … It was just like refreshing which is what we like to do. (Beni G, 2002)

Also important to The Mixologists is that their routines, like their club sets, incorporate a range of music that reflects their own musical interests, including hip-hop, drum and bass and reggae, giving the audience 'a little taste of everything' (Beni G, 2002). Beni G feels that this is encapsulated in the 2001 routine:

> … that's really the start of what it's all about – to define your sound. For us, that's basically putting whatever music we listen to, taking the best bits of that and stuff that'll work in routines and making a routine out of it. (Beni G, 2002)

Although the routine includes a variety of different sound samples and techniques it was important to the team that the techniques, especially scratching, were not the predominant element of the routine, but that they would 'compose a musical piece' which the audience would experience as a whole (Beni G, 2002).

Stage Two: Preliminary Rehearsals

- Discuss theme and end product
- Establish parameters for a constructive process

- Generate and share ideas
- Create and share material

The rehearsals began by members establishing the end product and how best to achieve their aims. In the case of The Mixologists' 2001 routine, both members were concerned with reflecting their own team identity and ability whilst also creating a routine which would be enjoyed by the audience, asking themselves, 'What do we want to do, what do we want to show people that we do – what's our music background or our influence ... what are the crowd going to like ...' (Beni G, 2002). The aspect of the crowd is extremely important to The Mixologists and any routine must both satisfy the crowd whilst correctly representing the team (Zaid). Beni G remarks that artistic decisions concerning what samples to use, how to put them together, as well as anticipating what the crowd will enjoy and react to, has become easier with experience:

> Sometimes for some people they might never quite know what they want, but for us, just from playing the club circuits and from being so into music, we know what works really well – or we think so anyway! ... We listen to so many different sorts of music that we can find stuff. We can hear samples, we hear bits in certain records and ... we just know straight away that'll smash it. In what particular way we'll put it together, we don't know how at that point, but we know we're going to use that in some way ... (Beni G, 2002)

Having created a number of routines and watched many others, Beni feels that the team has learnt what does and does not work and that this experience is drawn upon in the creation of the 2001 routine.

The Mixologists often have a vision of the routine before they begin the creative process. Before creating the 2001 routine, for example, the team knew that they wanted to make a routine where the members moved around. Though unsure at first how they could do this, they kept the idea in mind and finally managed to incorporate it into the performance (Beni G, 2002). During this stage, the team began to generate and share ideas and material. Beni G remarks that inspiration can come at any time – often whilst practicing but also during day-to-day activities such as watching television. At such times, the ideas are written down or specific records are placed in a designated record crate until they are needed. Before they even get to the turntables the members search through a lot of material, finding sounds that they want to use. Usually, one of two things acts as a catalyst for the routine at this stage – either a technique or a sound:

> Sometimes there'll be a technique, a way we do something with a certain sound which won't work, but if we pull out one of the other records that we like the sound of, it might work with that sound instead. (Beni G, 2002)

Beni believes that much of the material created at this stage arises by chance in the hours spent experimenting and practicing.

Stage Three: Phase 1 Rehearsals

- Establish structure and creative framework
- Create basic 'template'
- Generate material
- Try sections

The first main rehearsal phase began with the team establishing a creative framework within which to work. The Mixologist routine took around four weeks to create and within this, another timeframe was decided upon and worked to. The first three weeks included finding sounds, experimenting with sounds and techniques and generating and structuring the material. The final week was reserved for practicing the finished routine. Within this framework, especially within the first three weeks, the team like to incorporate some flexibility:

> No-one ever told us what to do or what not to do, so we just do what we normally do ... to have a target, but no real structured way of doing stuff so you don't limit yourself to certain angles or possibilities, basically. I really think it's good not to be too structured ... 'cos then you just lose sight of certain things that might be quite important. (Beni G, 2002)

At this stage in the creative process the Mixologist team met to share material and to experiment with that material together, forming it into larger sections. The basic structure of the routine was established. Every section of the routine was rigidly structured and did not allow for any improvisation. After the members chose what material to select and discard, they began to form a structure into which all the elements could be incorporated:

> ... now we've got all the bits we like we put it in a structure – how do we start it, how do we make the middle bit, how do we make it drop real good, how do we end it? And once we're at that stage it's like right, OK, 4 bars of this going boom – tss - boom – tss, then we'll go 4 bars and then you come in with the next bit and then after one quick drop out, of one bar or whatever, then we'll come in with everything or something like that – that's just an example, I'm just making it up, but that's how it would work basically. And then it would be like 4 bars of an outro/ending bit when we switch places every 2 bars and then that's it! So it is done to bars. (Beni G, 2003)

It is important to The Mixologists that the structure is formed after much of the experimentation and generation of ideas and material has taken place, to allow a full creative development:

... we don't think of it straight away because you need to get the ideas flowing, but once you've got all your ideas then its yea – structure it proper. Every single scratch. (Beni G, 2003)

The team even work on their actions and structure their behaviour and gesticulations:

Sometimes ... it's like we're in an acting class – I'm like, "you point here", and I'm going to go like that and you're going to go like that – it's crazy ... (Beni G, 2002)

Stage Four: Phase 2 Rehearsals

- Develop ideas and content
- Set and work on individual and group tasks
- Share with group
- Select and discard material
- Confirm content and clarify sections
- Reflect and evaluate
- Re-work according to feedback

The second rehearsal phase saw the team developing ideas and content through individual and group tasks, sharing results and selecting and discarding material. Beni G comments that the process of sharing the material, then selecting and discarding can be problematic. Members may bring many ideas and all could be rejected, causing friction in the team, but he feels that he and Go have established a good working relationship that deals with such situations:

It's almost like democracy in a certain way – if someone really doesn't like it that much you've got to question why ... A bit of pride gets in the way obviously, 'cos you think what you've got is good and then they turn around and say I'm not using that ... at the end of the day we talk through it now ... me and Go have got to the stage where we can really talk through it so it doesn't really get to the point where we want to punch each other out ... which obviously happens a lot! (Beni G, 2002)

Reflection and evaluation were ongoing throughout, concerning elements such as timescale, material and audience reception:

... it is on your mind quite a lot you're always thinking, 'are we going to get finished in time? We've got so much to do, is it really that good?'... when you're actually starting to build it and you know you've got a battle coming up, it is your mind a lot of the time ... there is an element of nervousness and of 'are people going to like it', are we going to be able to pull it off? (Beni G, 2002)

As they reached the final stages of the rehearsals, the team taped the routine and listened back to establish what worked well and what was more problematic and needed to be changed. Beni G reflected how this process gets quicker with experience and rather than persevering with an idea that is not working they will discard it and move on to another.

Phase 5: Final Rehearsals and Performance

- Rehearse and perform

The Mixologists set aside a week at the end of the creative process specifically for practice. During this time, they would practice everyday, repeatedly performing the six-minute routine. The reasons for this are two-fold. Firstly, to be confident in performance and secondly to enable them to practice what to do if a mistake is made during the performance, either from human or technical mishaps:

> ... you need to know how to recover ... you practice it loads and loads and you know how it should and shouldn't go ... if you skip a bit or the needle skips and you miss out a section – even like a bar – it's like man, you have to recover that, and like where do you start from, where do you pick up? (Beni G, 2002)

Beni G discusses how the team's experience enables him to cope with such a situation during the 2001 routine:

> ... you see me take the wrong record off ... I take one record off, go to take it away ... but I bring the same record back ... I look at my face and I didn't flinch, when I look at the video, but I know inside that I was thinking ... this has fucked me up and that's when I first made a mistake in the routine ... (Beni G, 2002)

The skill, he continues, is to know how to continue in such situations. It is only in such moments that improvisation is integrated into the routine.

3. Group Organisation

Both group members perform in all the sections. Although the size of the crew is relatively small they still use six turntables and four mixers between them and move between the equipment during the routine.

4. General Properties

The routine lasts for 5 minutes and 42 seconds and consists of six individual sections. The length of each section ranges from 32 seconds to one minute 24 seconds. The majority of sections are around one minute in length.

Table 9.5   Duration of individual sections within the routine

	Intro	Destiny	Do It	Reggae	Beep Melody	Drum and Bass	Total
Timing	32 secs	1 min 1 sec	1 min 8 secs	49 secs	48 secs	1 min 24 secs	5 mins 42 secs
Bar length	12 bars	28 bars	26 bars	15 bars	16 bars	32 bars	129 bars

All sections are in 4/4 time. There is some variation in both the 'Introduction' section, which has one bar in 6/4 time and the section 'Do It', which has one bar in 2/4 time.

Table 9.6   Time signature and tempo of sections

	Intro	Destiny	Do It	Reggae	Beep Melody	Bass and Drum
Time	4/4 1 bar 6/4	4/4 Time	4/4 Time 1 bar 2/4	4/4 Time	4/4 Time	4/4 Time
Tempo (bpm)	106 bpm 96 bpm bar 9 to end.	104 bpm Rall bar 25 to end.	92 bpm Rall bar 8–10 Original tempo resumed. Rall in final bar.	74 bpm Rall bar 7.	80 bpm	88 bpm (bars 1–16) 94 bpm (bars 17 on) Rall bars 4, 16 + 30.

Each section has a different tempo, ranging from 80 beats per minute to 106 beats per minute. The sections do contain some variation in tempo, either through a tempo change, as in 'Introduction', the use of rallentando, as in 'Destiny' 'Do It' and 'Reggae' or both, as in 'Bass and Drum'. Rallentandos are used both at the end of sections and within sections. In 'Destiny', 'Do It' and 'Bass and Drum', rallentandos are used at the end of the section to build tension and expectation for the next. However, in 'Do It, 'Reggae' and 'Bass and Drum', rallentandos are used during the section giving some punctuation between phrases or passages.

5. Sample Choice

The composition uses a total of 45 samples, fourteen vocal, 23 instrumental, two vocal and instrumental and six sound effects. Their division across the individual sections is as follows:

Table 9.7   Sample types used in the routine

	Instrumental	Instrumental and vocal	Sound effect	Textural	Vocal
Introduction	1	1	0	0	6
Destiny	4	0	1	0	3
Do It	7	0	1	0	2
Reggae	2	0	1	0	3
Beep Melody	5	1	1	0	0
Bass and Drum	4	0	2	0	0

Instrumental samples

The instrumental samples make up over half of sample types used in the routine and they are used in every section, forming the largest category type in four of the six sections. The instrumental samples used include guitar, bass, synthesizer, rhythmic scratch and drums. As well as these single samples, this section also uses instrumental samples with drums. The most used instrumental samples are basses, totalling eight. Three guitar samples are used, four drums and four instrumental and drum samples as well as two rhythm scratches and synthesizers.

Vocal samples

The vocal samples are the second largest category making up 31 per cent of all sample types used. They are only used in four of the six sections and their use diminishes throughout the routine, the final two sections, 'Beep Melody' and 'Bass and Drum' using none. Their prominence within individual sections alters, from 75 per cent of all samples in 'Introduction' to only 20 per cent in 'Do It'. All the vocal samples are spoken and all voices are male.

Vocal and instrumental samples

Two samples are used in the routine that contain vocals and instrumentation simultaneously. These occur in the 'Introduction' and 'Beep Melody' sections. In the 'Introduction', the sample is played solo. In Beep Melody however, the sample accompanies the other parts and becomes solo when the vocals enter. This category makes up only 5 per cent of total samples used.

Sound effects

Sound effect samples make up 13 per cent of all sample types used in the routine and appear in all sections excluding the 'Introduction'. The variety of sound effects is wide ranging, including electronically generated sounds such as static, to human sounds such as coughing and also a crashing sound. In all sections, sound effects are one of the smallest categories. Their greatest use is in the final section where they make up 33 per cent of all sample types used.

6. Structure

Each section is made up of between two and four smaller sections. The Introduction section is formed into two smaller sections, the first lasting for eight bars and the second for four. The three-section structure is the most popular form and is used in three of the main sections, 'Destiny', 'Beep Melody' and 'Bass and Drum'. However, the details of the form alter each time and the smaller sections do not follow any pattern in relation to length.

Table 9.8   Length of sections within the three-section structure

	Section A	Section B	Section C
Destiny	8 bars	12 bars	6 bars
Beep Melody	3 bars	8 bars	5 bars
Bass and Drum	8 bars	6 bars	8 bars

In 'Bass and Drum' the three-section structure is developed further, each section being preceded by a short segue, the first two lasting four bars and the third lasting two bars in length.

A four-section structure is used in 'Do It' and 'Reggae'. These sections consist of three smaller sections, one of which is developed. In 'Do It', these are performed in order, resulting in the form A, B, B1, C. In 'Reggae' they take a simple rondo form, with variation, A, B, A1, C. Whereas 'Do It' varies the section B, Reggae varies section A. Again, the lengths of these sections vary.

Table 9.9   Length of sections within the four-section structure

	A	A1	B	B1	C
Do It	4 bars		6 bars	8 bars	6 bars
Reggae	4 bars	1 bar	2 bars		8 bars

7. Sound Manipulation Techniques

The Mixologists use a variety of sound manipulation techniques. Both Beni G and Go use mixing, punchphasing, backspinning, scratching and pitch alteration. Go also uses record tapping.

Mixing

Mixing techniques are used in four of the six sections, 'Destiny', 'Do It', 'Beep Melody' and 'Bass and Drum'. Beni G and Go only use the technique to manipulate instrumental samples.

Punchphasing

The technique of punchphasing is used in all sections of the routine except 'Bass and Drum'. Beni G punchphases vocal samples, vocal and instrumental samples, instrumental samples and sound effects. Go also uses punchphasing techniques but uses only vocal samples and instrumental samples. Although Go punchphases in four of the five sections that use the technique he uses only approximately half the number of samples used by Beni G.

Backspinning

The technique of backspinning is used in all sections except 'Bass and Drum'. Beni G backspins vocal samples, vocal and instrumental samples and instrumental samples. Go backspins only instrumental samples.

Scratching

Scratch techniques are used in every section of the routine. Both members scratch vocal samples, instrumental samples and sound effect samples but only Go scratches vocal and instrumental samples. Go is the only member to scratch in the Introduction.

Pitch alteration

Beni G uses two techniques to alter pitch, firstly by resetting the rpm button and secondly by moving the pitch regulator. Each of these techniques is used only once, in the section 'Bass and Drum'.

Record tapping

Go creates a two-bar repeated rhythmic pattern not using a sample from a record, but by creating a sound from the record itself. The needle is placed on the record that is not spinning and when the finger taps the vinyl it creates a short sound. Go uses this sound to create a two-bar rhythm, repeated twice. This technique is used solely by Go in the 'Bass and Drum' section.

As is apparent from the information above, some of the techniques are shared, while only one group member takes others on. In their uses of the techniques, each group member is either a primary user – a group member who uses the technique frequently; a secondary user – a group member who used the technique, but less frequently than the primary user; or a minimal user – a group member who uses the technique very infrequently.

Table 9.10   The Mixologists: Manipulation techniques and their users

	Beni G	Go
Punchphasing vocal samples	Primary	Secondary
Punchphasing vocal and instrumental samples	Primary	
Punchphasing instrumental samples	Primary	Primary
Punchphasing sound effects samples	Primary	
Backspinning vocal samples	Primary	
Backspinning vocal and instrumental samples	Primary	
Backspinning instrumental samples	Secondary	Primary
Backspinning sound effect samples	Primary	Minimal
Scratching vocal samples	Primary	
Scratching vocal and instrumental samples	Secondary	
Scratching instrumental samples	Primary	
Scratching sound effect samples	Primary	
Mixing vocal samples		
Mixing vocal and instrumental samples		
Mixing instrumental samples	Secondary	Primary
Mixing sound effect samples		
Pitch alteration – reset rpm button	Primary	
Pitch alteration – move pitch regulator	Primary	
Record tapping		Primary

Key

Primary user of technique	(dark shading)
Secondary user of technique	(medium shading)
Minimal use of technique	(light shading)

It is evident from the table that Beni G is the sole primary user of punchphasing vocal and instrumental samples and sound effects as well as pitch alteration techniques. Go is the sole primary user of scratch vocal and instrumental samples and record tapping techniques. Beni G is a secondary user of the techniques of backspinning and mixing instrumental samples whilst Go is a secondary user of punchphasing vocal samples. The team members share primary use of four techniques – punchphasing instrumental samples and scratching techniques using vocal samples, instrumental samples and sound effects.

8. Texture

The texture of the routine varies from sections that are relatively light in texture, to those where the texture is more substantial and to those where the texture changes throughout the section. In the 'Introduction' and 'Reggae' sections, the texture is relatively thin. However, the sample use, content and relationship between parts are different in each. In 'Introduction', each sample is heard in turn and most samples consist of only a single sound. The final sample is made up of a number of simultaneous sounds but it plays solo. In contrast, in 'Reggae' some of the instrumental samples used consist of a number of sounds heard simultaneously. However, although four turntables are used in this section no more than two are used at any one time. In 'Introduction', where both members perform, the texture is created between them. All parts are equally audible but the vocals are more prevalent. In 'Reggae' however, the parts fall into roles of main part and accompaniment. Go has a strong repeated melody line that Beni provides fills for or accompanies. Beni G has a solo line at the end. In contrast, in the section 'Destiny' the texture is dense as many of the samples used are low in register and are used simultaneously. For the majority of the section all parts are equally important and parts fit together to make a phrase. All parts are equally audible except the drum that has a more accompaniment role. The thickness of texture is partly due to the fact that in the most part both musicians perform together, solo sections only evident where the other member needs to change record.

In the sections 'Do It', 'Beep Melody' and 'Bass and Drum', the texture changes throughout the section. In 'Do It' and 'Beep Melody' the lighter textures are due to parts being heard in turn and samples consisting of solo sounds. In 'Bass and Drum' the texture is thin where Beni G performs the segues alone. In all three of these sections, the texture becomes heavier where both members play simultaneously, either where patterns are shared or when one part accompanies the other. In 'Beep Melody' this is intensified by the use of a multi sound sample and in 'Bass and Drum' because many of the samples are low in register.

In all three sections, the relationships between parts change. In 'Do It', the members begin by performing the phrase between them, each equally important. The relationship then changes to parts being in the foreground and background before returning to equal importance where the phrase is again shared. In 'Beep Melody', the parts begin as equally important then change to solo and accompaniment before becoming just a solo. In 'Bass and Drum' Beni G has a more prominent part, either playing solo or being accompanied by Go.

The Scratch Perverts Routine, New York, September 1999

1. Context

This routine was created by the London-based turntable team the Scratch Perverts; Tony Vegas, Prime Cuts, Mr Thing and First Base. The routine was made for performance at the 1999 DMC Team Championships at the Hammerstein Ballroom, New York City in September 1999, where twelve turntable teams from around the world competed to become the first world team champions. The notation and analysis has been completed using video footage of the performance, published by DMC (1999) and interviews given by the team members.

2. The Process of Collective Creation

Stage One: Pre-devising Administration

- Team building
- Establish the working parameters of the group
- Allocation of roles
- Establish skills of individuals
- Establish common artistic ground

For the Scratch Perverts team 'pre-devising administration' occurred prior to the creation of the 1999 DMC routine as team members were already working creatively together. The working parameters of the group were in place, individual skills were known and common artistic ground was established.

Stage Two: Preliminary Rehearsals

- Discuss theme and end product
- Establish parameters for a constructive process
- Generate and share ideas
- Create and share material

Prime Cuts describes how ideas for the routine can be generated anywhere, at any time, both individually and with others:

> ... you just stumble across it ... it just pops into your head – you might be in the bath or having a shower or eating crisps at home or something and the idea just comes to you, or you're having a conversation with somebody that just sparks an idea. (Scratch Perverts, 2000)

These ideas are then shared and developed within the team, a process which is explained by Plus One who has witnessed the creation of Scratch Perverts routines:

... they were experimenting ... and I was just like, hold on, try that, try this, so they started practising other stuff ... we're all feeding so many ideas ... watching musicians jam together and then just suddenly this thing arrives which with a little bit of fine tuning became ... what I thought was genius as a routine. (Plus One)

Stages Three and Four: Phase 1 and 2 Rehearsals

- Establish structure and creative framework
- Create basic 'template'
- Generate material
- Try sections
- Develop ideas and content
- Set and work on individual and group tasks
- Share with group
- Select and discard material
- Confirm content and clarify sections
- Reflect and evaluate
- Re-work according to feedback

For the Scratch Perverts, the creative process is a lengthy one. Prime Cuts comments that it may take up to 60 hours to create one minute of a routine, comparing this to the creative processes of animators:

Constructively a battle is like animating a cartoon, it's like frame by frame and the difference between the creation of a piece and listening to a piece is pretty much proportionate to animation. (MajikFist, 2004)

Tony Vegas explains how a number of frameworks may be created which are then adapted to suit individual members. These changes can cause friction in the team:

It leads to a lot of arguments ... there's a lot of strong personalities in one room. And I'm a stubborn bastard the way they all are ... It's tense because it's very much a working relationship. (Vegas)

The framework must allow for all team members to input into the process:

... there's definitely, definitely, definitely not one person saying "Right. We'll do this, you do that", I mean, that's just not going to happen. I don't think that's any way to work musically when you've got four people trying to come up with something. (Wax Factor, 1999)

The process itself is split between trying out particular ideas suggested by team members and improvising as a group. These ideas would be developed to create a section, which would then lead to the creation of the next:

> Someone might say, "Right. I've got this really good idea, shall we give it a go?" That's how, I'd say, about 50 per cent of the routine came up, and then the other 50 per cent was just us jamming. We'd do something and be like "Oh no, hang on. No, that's good" and then that'd snowball into something else which would snowball into something else and then, hey, you've got a minute and a half of a routine and then you blend it into another idea and so on so forth. (Wax Factor, 1999)

Phase 5: Final Rehearsals and Performance

• Rehearse and perform

The Scratch Perverts do not refer directly to a rehearsal phase in the creation of this routine, but when interviewed at Scratchcon 2000, Tony Vegas does refer to a specific period of rehearsal in the creation of routines in general:

> ... it's hard work and the idea is that you create six minutes of music that is rehearsed, that is performed like a piece of music, is performed in a band or an orchestra or anything. (Scratch Perverts, 2000)

3. Group Organisation

All members of the crew perform in five of the six sections, though in section two, 'Rock', First Base has little input. Mr Thing does not perform in the 'Introduction'. Positions change very little, team members tending to use the same turntables and mixers throughout. All team members use at least one turntable and mixer; Tony Vegas and Prime Cuts use two turntables each. First Base uses turntable number one and mixer number one; Tony Vegas uses turntables two and three and mixer number two; Prime Cuts uses turntables four and five and mixer three, and Mr Thing uses turntable six and mixer four. This set-up varies slightly in three sections of the piece. In the Introduction and Rock sections Tony Vegas and Prime Cuts use only one turntable each; turntables three and four remain unused. In the 'Introduction', the non-participation of Mr Thing means that turntable six and mixer four are unused. In the Finale section, members perform on their usual turntables for the majority of the section but for a short amount of time move between, resulting in all members utilizing all the equipment.

4. General Properties

The routine consists of six smaller sections and lasts for 6 minutes and 11 seconds. The single sections range from 10 seconds to 1 minute 55 seconds in length. However, the majority of sections are around 1 minute long.

Table 9.11   Duration of individual sections within the routine

Introduction	Rock	Allies	Word	Melody	Finale	Total
10 secs	1 min	1 min 10 secs	1 min 4 secs	50 secs	1 min 57 secs	6 mins 11 secs

All the sections are in 4/4 time. There is some slight variation in 'Rock' which contains one bar in 3/4 and 'Allies', which contains one bar in 5/4. Each section has a different tempo that is retained throughout the section, except for the 'Finale' where there are tempo changes within the section. The differences in tempo between the other sections is not great, varying from 'Melody', the slowest at 93 beats per minute, to the fastest, 'Introduction' and 'Rock' which are both at 108 beats per minute. Although there are no definite tempo changes within these sections the tempo in the Allies section is pulled around due to the use of pauses and the very slight speed variations between the large numbers of samples, especially vocal samples, used. The tempo in the 'Finale' section alters five times and gives the greatest variation in tempo of the whole piece, the slowest being 86 beats per minute and the quickest being 126 beats per minute.

Table 9.12   Time signature and tempo of sections

	Introduction	Rock	Allies	Word	Melody	Finale
Time	4/4	4/4 One bar 3/4	4/4 One bar 5/4	4/4	4/4	4/4
Tempo (bpm)	108	108	103	96	93	Bars 1–12 = 124 Bars 14–27 = 86 Bars 19–22 = 120 Bars 24–30 = 126 Bars 31–38 = 93

5. Sample Choice

The composition uses a total of 48 samples, 26 vocal, 18 instrumental and four sound effects.

Table 9.13   Sample types used in the routine

	Instrumental	Instrumental and vocal	Sound effect	Textural	Vocal
Introduction	1	0	0	0	4
Rock	1	0	0	0	6
Allies	2	0	4	0	10
Word	4	0	0	0	2
Melody	4	0	0	0	0
Finale	6	0	0	0	4

Instrumental samples
The instrumental samples make up 38 per cent of all samples used and their use builds throughout the routine. The 'Introduction' and the 'Rock' sections use only one instrumental sample each, two are used in the 'Allies', four in the 'Word' and 'Melody' sections, rising to six in the 'Finale'. The instrumental samples are second in importance in the first three sections but for the final three sections become the most frequently used. The 'Melody' section sees their greatest use, being the only sample type used in that section. The instrumental samples used include guitars, bass lines, strings, instrumental stabs and drums. The most used are drum samples that make up nine out of the 18 different instrumental samples in total. The second largest group is bass samples (four), followed by instrumental stabs (three) and finally guitar samples (two).

Vocal samples
Vocal samples are the largest category, making up 54 per cent of all samples used. Their use across the sections ranges from none in the melody section to 10 in the Allies section. The highest percentage use of all samples used in one section is in 'Rock', where 86 per cent of the samples are vocal. The vocal samples are the most frequently used in the first three sections, but in the final three sections become second in importance. Although the samples range in length and content all are samples of male voices speaking.

Sound effect samples
Sound effect samples make up only 8 per cent of total samples used and are used only in the 'Allies' section. Three of the four samples; the crying baby, gunshot and plane crash are simply punchphased and the sample sound is not manipulated. The plane engine is the only sound effect sample used that is manipulated, through scratch techniques, to enhance the effect of the sample.

6. Structure

Each section is made up of phrases that are repeated, often with variation. The length of phrases differs from section to section from only one bar (in the 'Introduction' section), to two bars (in the 'Melody') section and four bars (the 'Rock', 'Allies' and 'Word' sections.) The Finale is made up of phrases of both one bar and four bars in length. These phrases are often repeated, usually with some variation and all sections except the 'Introduction' use more than one phrase. The number of phrases and their repetition and variation alters from section to section.

Introduction
A one-bar phrase is repeated with some variation four times.

Rock
This section is made up of six blocks, each a four-bar phrase. Elements of this four-bar phrase are repeated. Variation means that the parts of each musician gradually change throughout the section. At least one aspect of the previous block is retained in the next. This section contains some call and response.

Allies
This is the only section that is divided into two contrasting parts, both of equal length. The second section does not follow a repeated phrase pattern, as the narrative nature of the section dictates the structure. However, the first section does follow a phrase-led structure, taking the form of a four bar phrase, repeated with variation four times.

Word
This is the first section to use more than one phrase, repeated. Although it still relies on repeated phrases it uses two in a kind of ternary form; A, A1, B, B, B, A2. A four-bar phrase is played (A) which is then is repeated with variation (A1). A different four-bar phrase is then repeated three times (B). The first four-bar phrase then returns, again with some variation (A2).

Melody
This section returns to a very simple two-bar phrase, repeated with variation 10 times.

Finale
The largest number of different phrases is evident in the 'Finale' section where five different phrases are used, divided by small segue sections. Four different four-bar phrases and one one-bar phrase are used in this section, and unlike the section 'Word', none are returned to, forming the structure; A, A1, A2, Segue, B, Segue, B1, Segue, B2, B3, C, D, E. A is a four-bar phrase repeated 3 times with variation. B is a four-bar phase repeated four times with variation. C is a one-bar phrase repeated eight times. D and E are both four-bar phrases, played only once. This structure is made slightly more complex by the inclusion of three small segue sections between these phrases.

7. Sound Manipulation Techniques

The Scratch Perverts use four main sound manipulation techniques – punchphasing, backspinning, scratching and beat juggling. Tony Vegas and Prime Cuts are the only team members to beat juggle.

Punchphasing
Punchphasing occurs in all section of the routine. All team members punchphase vocal samples and instrumental samples throughout the section. Tony Vegas, Prime Cuts and Mr Thing also punchphase sound effects.

Backspinning
Like punchphasing, backspinning occurs in all sections of the routine. All members backspin vocal samples and instrumental samples. No sound effect sample is backspun.

Scratching
Scratching techniques are used in every section of the routine. Prime Cuts scratches non-specific samples (those where the resulting scratch sound, rather than the original sample, is the important aspect), vocal samples and instrumental samples. Tony Vegas scratches vocal samples and instrumental samples. Mr Thing and First Base only scratch instrumental samples. No sound effects are scratched.

Beat juggling
Beat juggling techniques are used only in the 'Word' and 'Melody' sections. Prime Cuts and Tony Vegas beat juggle vocal samples in 'Word' and instrumental samples in 'Melody'.

As is apparent from the information above, some of the techniques are shared, while only one group member takes others on. In their uses of the techniques each group members is either a primary user – a group member who uses the technique frequently; a secondary user – a group member who used the technique, but less frequently than the primary user; or a minimal user – a group member who uses the technique very infrequently.

Table 9.14   The Scratch Perverts: Manipulation techniques and their users

	First Base	Tony Vegas	Prime Cuts	Mr Thing
Punchphasing vocal samples	Primary	Secondary	Secondary	Minimal
Punchphasing instrumental samples	Primary	Minimal		
Punchphasing sound effect samples		Primary	Primary	Primary
Backspinning vocal samples	Secondary	Primary	Primary	Minimal
Backspinning instrumental samples	Primary	Secondary	Minimal	Secondary
Backspinning sound effect samples				
Scratching non-specific samples			Primary	
Scratching vocal samples		Primary	Primary	
Scratching instrumental samples	Minimal	Secondary	Minimal	Primary
Scratching sound effect samples				
Beat Juggling vocal samples		Primary	Primary	
Beat Juggling instrumental samples		Primary	Primary	
Beat Juggling sound effects				

Key

Primary user of technique	Primary (dark)
Secondary user of technique	Secondary (medium grey)
Minimal use of technique	Minimal (light grey)

First Base is a primary user of punchphasing techniques using vocal and instrumental samples and backspinning techniques using instrumental samples. He is a secondary user of backspinning techniques using vocal samples. He is a minimal user of scratching using instrumental samples. He does not use any other techniques. Tony Vegas is a primary user of punchphasing techniques using sound effects and backspinning using vocal samples. He is also a primary user of scratching techniques using vocal samples and beat juggling techniques, using both vocal and instrumental samples. He is a secondary user of punchphasing techniques using vocal samples and both backspinning and scratching techniques using instrumental samples. Tony Vegas is a minimal user of punchphasing techniques using instrumental samples. Prime Cuts is a primary user of punchphasing techniques using sound effects and backspinning techniques using vocal samples. He is also a primary user of scratching techniques using both non-specific and vocal samples.

He is a primary user of beat juggling techniques using both vocal and instrumental samples. Prime Cuts is a secondary user of punchphasing techniques using vocal samples. He is a minimal user of backspinning and scratching techniques using instrumental samples. Mr Thing is a primary user of the punchphasing technique using sound effects and scratching techniques using instrumental samples. He is a secondary user of punchphasing and backspinning techniques using instrumental samples. He is a minimal user of punchphasing and backspinning techniques using vocal samples.

Prime Cuts is the only individual to use the technique of scratching non-specific samples. This is the only technique that is used by only one team member. All the other techniques are shared. A number of group members share primary techniques, whether because they are commonly used techniques or because they are linked to pair and group work when building a phrase together, for example punchphasing and backspinning sound effects, scratching vocal samples and beat juggling. Although many techniques are shared, some group members are the sole primary user for a technique, pointing to their specialism, for example First Base punchphasing vocal samples and Prime Cuts scratching. All of the members display a minimal use of techniques at some point during the routine but these are always with techniques that also are primary or secondary techniques of other members.

8. Texture

In some of the sections, namely 'Introduction' and 'The Allies', all parts are equally important. None of the team members can be seen as having the main part, but instead musicians construct the phrases and section together, parts joining in turn to create a through-line. In these sections, there is little sense of foreground or background. In the other sections, members tend to pair up to provide either the main part or the accompaniment. 'Rock' is constructed through the relationship between Prime Cuts and Tony Vegas. The pair share the foreground and Mr Thing provides the background. In the 'Word' section this pairing strategy is again evident, Tony Vegas and Prime Cuts both providing the main parts and First Base and Mr Thing providing the accompaniment. In the 'Melody' section which follows, these pairings are reversed and First Base and Mr Thing provide the main melody line while Tony Vegas and Prime Cuts provide the accompaniment. In the 'Finale', the prominence of the parts changes. Prime Cuts, Mr Thing and First Base all have solo lines but overall there is still a divide between those musicians who have a prominent role and those who have a supporting role. Once more, Tony Vegas and Prime Cuts create the main thrust of the section and First Base and Mr Thing accompany this. However, in the alternating section where the musicians move between turntables and mixers all sections are equally important in creating the through-line.

The overall texture of sections alters throughout the routine. 'Introduction' and 'Allies' are relatively thin when compared to the heavier textures of 'Rock' and

'Word'. Some sections retain a texture throughout; for example, 'Introduction', which is thin throughout and 'Word', which is relatively thick throughout. The 'Rock' section builds in texture as parts are added. 'Melody' changes between lighter passages, where First Base and Mr Thing perform alone, and denser passages where they are accompanied by Tony Vegas and Prime Cuts. In the 'Finale' section, containing solos, duets, trios and quartets, the texture also varies, thin solo passages contrasting with thick ensemble passages. The different textural quality of sections is partly determined by the number of team members playing at any one time. In the 'Allies' section, for example, more than two members rarely play at a time. In contrast, in 'Word', which is relatively thick in texture, at least three members play simultaneously throughout.

Characteristics and Comparisons

Firstly, characteristics of the compositional processes of team turntable composition evident in the process of collective creation will be discussed and then those evident in the completed artistic product, the routine.

The Process of Collective Creation

The discussion of the process of team formation and the collective creation of the routines result in the development of a number of characteristics of the collective creation of hip-hop turntable teams.

1. The routines are created through a devising process　　What is clear from the discussion of the creation of team routines through the devising framework is that all the teams do exhibit characteristics of each stage of the devising process.

2. All three teams work within a similar devising framework　　Each team creates the routine within the flexible devising framework that was established.

3. Details within the devising framework differ from team to team　　Although each team creates within the devising framework, there are variations from team to team. For all three teams, stage one, pre-devising administration, occurred prior to the collective creation of the routines. In stage two, all three teams generate, create and share ideas but their methods of doing this vary. The Mixologists and the Scratch Perverts describe how this often happens away from the turntables, even whilst undertaking everyday activities, but the DMU Crew take a more hands-on turntable-based approach. In stage three, all three teams begin to establish creative frameworks and structure their routines but, again, do so different ways. The Scratch

Perverts create a number of frameworks that are then adapted to suit individual members. The DMU Crew decide on a framework and then generate material to put in it, the structure then developing alongside the material. The Mixologists, however, only form a structure after they have experimented fully and generated material, as they do not want the structure to shape the creative development. In stage four, all teams display characteristics of the cycle of development and evaluation, the 'devising loop'. All continue to develop ideas and content both individually and as a group. Again, this is achieved in different ways. The Scratch Perverts, for example, try out ideas and improvise as a group, developing through practical application. The DMU Crew on the other hand, develop mostly through discussion and then try out what they have decided. For all teams, reflection and evaluation is ongoing throughout, covering aspects such as timescale, material, and reception, and are inextricably linked to other elements of the phase. For The Mixologists this sometimes takes place through recording the routine and listening back to it, but for the other two teams it is mostly through discussion following practice runs. All three teams describe the final stage of rehearsing the routine as a distinct phase both to build general confidence and to develop a range of approaches to deal with any mistakes.

4. The devising framework is used unconsciously   The three turntable teams have developed their compositional processes in isolation from the practices of traditional western art and do not work in artistic environments where they would be aware of devising as a creative model. Their use of this creative process is not a conscious artistic decision, rejecting other creative models, but rather the most natural process to achieve the desired artistic product. Beni G reflects:

> ... it's just something that I don't ever think or talk about ... It's just like, that's what we do – we get together and we do it, and Go won't be like, "Oh, this is great that we've spent so much time looking for samples that we're now ready at week three to go on to the next stage", is just don't work like that! ... When you swim you jump in the pool, move your arms, go to the end and get out. It's the same with us. We'll go into rehearsal, we get our records, we fuck about, we get some ideas, we might write them down, we go home, whatever. It's like a process we go through and you never think about it until you're asked for it. (Beni G, 2002)

For the DMU Crew, The Mixologists and the Scratch Perverts, devising is not an imposed process but occurs naturally through the social nature of the teams and sharing of skills and ideas. The artistic team is formed through friendships and acquaintances coming together to share common interests and goals as well as ideas and techniques resulting in the collective creation of a routine.

The Artistic Product

In each category of the analysis the teams display some major similarities which are presented here as characteristics.

1. The routines do not allow for improvisation   Each routine is strictly structured and rehearsed.

2. The routines consist of a number of smaller sections   Both The Mixologists and the Scratch Perverts structure their routines in a similar way. Both routines consist of a short introduction followed by five longer sections, the first four of these are around a minute long and the final section is longer – 1 minute 34 seconds in the Mixologist routine and 1 minute 57 seconds in the Scratch Perverts routine. The overall structure of the DMU Crew routine differs from this and the routine consists instead of three sections ranging from 2 minutes 48 seconds to 4 minutes 44 seconds in length.

3. All sections are in 4/4 time except for minor deviations   All sections of all three routines are in 4/4 time. There are small exceptions to this in the routines of the Scratch Perverts and The Mixologists which both include isolated bars of different time signatures, used either to accommodate the extra length of a vocal or sound effect sample or to build anticipation.

4. Tempos alter in most sections   The tempos used by the teams in their routines mostly alter every section, the Scratch Perverts being the only team to keep a tempo in consecutive sections. Once the DMU Crew have established a tempo they stick to it rigidly, but the Scratch Perverts include pauses and The Mixologists include frequent rallentandos.

5. Teams use a range of samples, some of which are team specific   Between them, the turntable teams use five different sample types. These are used in different ways and have different degrees of prevalence. The three teams all use vocal samples and instrumental samples. The Mixologists and the Scratch Perverts both also use sound effect samples. The Mixologists alone use vocal and instrumental samples and only the DMU Crew use atmospheric samples.

For both the DMU Crew and The Mixologists, instrumental samples make up the largest sample category used in the routines. The types of instrumental samples differ from team to team. All three teams use drum and bass samples. Both The Mixologists and the Scratch Perverts use guitar samples. As well as having sample sounds in common, the teams also use instrumental sounds that are not used by the others. The DMU Crew, for example, use samples of single tones, The Mixologists use synthesizer samples and a scratch rhythm and the Scratch Perverts use instrumental stabs. The prevalence of instrumental samples in individual sections also differs from team to team, though all sections in all three routines contain some.

For the Scratch Perverts, vocal samples are the largest sample category used. For both the DMU Crew and The Mixologists, vocal samples are only the second largest category. Every vocal sample used by all three teams is a spoken male voice.

The Mixologists and the Scratch Perverts both use sound effect samples. This sample category is only used in some of the sections and is never the main sample type in any section. In both routines the category includes both traditional sound effects like a crash or a plane sound as well as human vocal sounds such as an 'agh' or a baby crying. The Mixologists also use electronically generated sound effects.

The Mixologists are the only team to use vocal and instrumental samples but they are a minor part, only being used twice in the whole routine. The DMU Crew is the only team to use atmospheric samples and these are restricted to the first section, 'Texture' and make up only 10 per cent of all the samples used by the team.

The DMU Crew create their routine using only 20 different samples, compared to The Mixologists who use 45 and the Scratch Perverts who use 48. Conversely, the DMU Crew routine is double the duration of either of the others who therefore use twice as many samples in half the time. The DMU Crew get more from fewer samples because of the prevalence of layering techniques in their routine and because samples change infrequently. The Mixologists and the Scratch Perverts have a much higher turnover of samples as, although their routines are not always quicker in tempo, sample changes occur more often. For The Mixologists, this is compounded by the fact that there are only two team members, meaning that each team member has to deal with nearly twice as many samples as each member of the Scratch Perverts team and over four times as may as the DMU Crew members.

6. Teams use the same techniques in different ways   The three teams use many similar sound manipulation techniques. All three teams use punchphasing, backspinning and scratching techniques but the prevalence of these techniques throughout the routines differs from team to team. Only the DMU Crew and The Mixologists use mixing techniques but the technique is not used with either vocal samples or sound effects. Instead, the technique is mostly used to mix instrumental samples and, in the case of the DMU Crew, atmospheric samples. Beat juggling techniques are used only by the Scratch Perverts to manipulate vocal samples and instrumental samples equally. This technique is not widely used but is central to the two sections where it is used. For the DMU Crew punchphasing vocal samples is the most common use of the technique, followed by punchphasing instrumental samples. For the Scratch Perverts and The Mixologists, punchphasing vocal samples and instrumental samples are also both central techniques, The Mixologists being the only team to punchphase vocal and instrumental samples.

Whereas punchphasing sound effects is used by The Mixologists in half of the sections of their routine, for the Scratch Perverts it is a minor technique and it is never used by the DMU Crew. In the routines of The Mixologists and the Scratch Perverts, backspinning instrumental samples is a central technique and, in the case of the Scratch Perverts, backspinning vocal samples as well. This technique is used less by the DMU Crew. The Mixologists are the only team to use this technique to manipulate vocal and instrumental samples and sound effect samples, and even then, its use is minimal. Scratching instrumental samples is prevalent in the routines of The Mixologists and Scratch Perverts but is less used by the DMU Crew. The DMU Crew and Mixologists also scratch vocal samples, a technique not used as much by the Scratch Perverts. The Scratch Perverts are the only team to scratch non-specific samples and The Mixologists are the only team to scratch sound effects.

7. Some techniques are specific to particular teams   Only the DMU Crew uses sticker-looping techniques. Although the technique is not widely used, it is central to the section in which it appears. The DMU Crew are also alone in their use of a technique to create a rhythm by tapping the audio signal cable, connected to a mixer. The Mixologists use techniques that in these routines are particular to them – pitch alteration and record tapping. Whilst they are not central techniques, they do add interest to the sections they are in.

8. Roles, responsibilities and techniques are shared between group members   The roles and responsibilities of individual group members in their use of specific sound manipulation techniques differ from team to team. In their uses of the techniques, each group members is either a primary user – a group member who uses the technique frequently, a secondary user – a group member who used the technique, but less frequently than the primary user, usually in a support role, or a minimal user – a group member who uses the technique very infrequently. In the DMU Crew, members are mainly primary users of techniques and tend to have sole responsibility for those techniques assigned to them. Only three techniques have secondary user support. In the Mixologist team, each member is responsible for a number of different techniques and less than half of these are shared between members. Team members are rarely secondary users of techniques as there are only two members to create the routine over six turntables. In order to create the routine with so few members they are usually primary users, either alone or simultaneously. In the Scratch Perverts team, two members, Prime Cuts and Tony Vegas, are the two main primary users of techniques and share the majority of these. The other team members adopt those not covered by them. As there are four members creating the routine over six turntables they can support through the secondary use of techniques to a greater extent than The Mixologists. They also display a greater secondary use of techniques than the DMU Crew. Approximately half the techniques are used in one degree or another by at least three or more members. Members of the Scratch Perverts are the only musicians across the three teams to display a minimal use of some techniques, reflecting the spread of techniques used across the team.

9. Common structures for the smaller sections are layering, binary and chain form   The three teams use a number of different structural approaches within the individual sections, some shared and some particular to a specific team. The DMU Crew use layering techniques, The Mixologists use mostly progressive chain form as well as some binary form and the Scratch Perverts use a mixture of layering and binary, progressive chain and rondo form.

The DMU Crew use layering as their main structural technique in all the sections. Rather than being strictly structured, the sections are formed around a pre-agreed framework that is reliant on cues. Following sound cues, members introduce different sample layers that play together before being removed. The sections develop gradually with the inclusion and exclusion of the layers that give different combinations of parts. This structural approach is also evident in the 'Rock' section of the Scratch Perverts' routine. Here, repeated phrases change gradually throughout the section, each time one aspect of the last phrase is continued into the next.

Both The Mixologists and the Scratch Perverts use binary form. In The Mixologists' routine it is used in the 'Introduction' section that consists of two smaller sections, the first of eight bars and the second of four bars. In the Scratch Perverts' routine it is evident in the longer 'Allies' section that consists of two contrasting parts of equal length. Across the three routines, there is only one example of a phrase being returned to later in a section, in a simple rondo form. This is only evident in the 'Word' section of the Scratch Perverts routine where the first phrase returns to end the section as a developed repetition.

Both The Mixologists and the Scratch Perverts also use chain form. Whereas it is only used once in the Scratch Perverts routine, it is used to structure five of The Mixologists sections. This chain form takes two different forms. Firstly it is used in a very simple way in The Mixologists' sections 'Destiny', 'Beep Melody' and 'Bass and Drum' sections, where three smaller sections, A, B and C are played consecutively. In the section 'Do It' and 'Reggae' this form is developed to include repeated variations of the initial phrases but these always directly follow the original phase, for example A. B, B1 and C (in 'Do It') and A, A1, B and C (in 'Reggae'). This form is also used in the Scratch Perverts section 'Finale', though here it is developed further. Here, five different sections are heard, two repeated with variation and further developed by the inclusion of short segues; A, A1, A2, Segue, B, Segue, B1, Segue, B2, B3, C, D and E.

10. The different sections across all three routines show different relationships between parts, some of which are shared and others that are particular to specific teams   There are four main relationships demonstrated in the routines;

- No one part is more prominent than another, each part being equal in the texture.
- The parts play in turn to create a passage between them.
- The parts take the roles of foreground (solo) and background (accompaniment).
- Members pair up to create a part between them.

A number of sections contain combinations of these main relationships. The most frequent relationship across all three routines is that of parts playing in turn to create passages between team members, and the combination of this with relationship of main part and accompaniment. In The Mixologists routine, this is evident in the sections 'Destiny' and it is also well demonstrated by the Scratch Perverts in 'Rock'. The second most common relationship is the combination of two members pairing up to create a passage simultaneously, combined with the relationship of a main part and accompaniment. This relationship is used in the Scratch Perverts' sections 'Word', 'Melody' and 'Finale'. Although this is a common relationship between parts in the Scratch Perverts' routine it is not used much by any of the other teams. Pairing up is used by The Mixologists, as there are only two of them it is difficult to establish if this is through choice or necessity! The final two relationship types used are each part being equal in the creation of the texture and the relationship of main part and accompaniment and these are both evident in two sections. Each part being equal in creating a texture is used in the first two DMU Crew sections, 'Texture' and 'Click and Clap', but is not used by the other two teams. The relationship of parts divided into main part and accompaniment, not combined with any other relationship, is used in two sections of the Mixologist routine, 'Reggae' and 'Bass and Drum', but not by any of the other teams.

11. Texture varies throughout the sections of the routines   The individual sections of the three different routines fall into three basic categories – those that are predominantly thin in texture, those that are predominantly thick in texture and those where the texture changes during the section. Thinner textures and those sections that change in texture are most common in the routines, each team creating only one section that has a predominantly thick texture. The Mixologists and the Scratch Perverts routines both contain three where the texture changes, two that are predominantly light and one that is predominantly heavy. The textures in the DMU Crew routine, however, do not change greatly within the sections. Across all three routines, the texture is not determined solely by the types of samples used, all sample types being evident in the creation of a range of textures. This is excluding sections that are predominantly made of vocal samples, which tend to have a lighter texture, for example the 'Introduction' and 'Allies' section of the Scratch Perverts routine.

All teams create sections that are relatively light in texture. The sections use a variety of sample types including those constructed from predominantly instrumental samples, those predominantly vocal and those that use instrumental and vocal samples equally. For the DMU Crew these are 'Click and Clap' and 'Bass and Scratch'; for The Mixologists 'Introduction' and 'Reggae'; and for the Scratch Perverts 'Introduction' and 'Allies'. In the majority of cases, this texture is partly created as the samples used are of a single sound, for example a single instrumental sample or a solo vocal sample. In three of the sections, The Mixologists' 'Introduction' and the Scratch Perverts' 'Introduction' and 'Allies', this is increased by the way in which the majority of samples are performed in turn rather than simultaneously. In the DMU Crew section 'Bass and Scratch' and The Mixologists' 'Reggae', although parts may play together, there are rarely more than two parts simultaneously.

All teams create one section that is relatively dense in texture. For the DMU Crew this is 'Texture', for The Mixologists, 'Destiny' and for the Scratch Perverts, 'Word'. These sections use a variety of sample types, including those that are constructed using predominantly atmospheric samples and those that use instrumental and vocal samples equally. In the sections by the DMU Crew and The Mixologists, the density of texture is partly due to the low register and tonal qualities of many of the samples used. In all three sections, parts are heard together with all members performing simultaneously, especially in the Scratch Perverts' routine where the beat juggling technique used allows the samples to be repeated seamlessly without any gaps.

The Mixologists and The Scratch Perverts both include three sections in their routine where the texture varies. For The Mixologists these sections are 'Do It', 'Beep Melody' and 'Bass and Drum' and for the Scratch Perverts they are 'Rock', 'Melody' and 'Finale'. These sections include a variety of sample types ranging from those that predominantly use instrumental or vocal samples to those that use both equally. In the majority of the sections the lighter textures are caused by the use of single note samples, solo passages by team members or both. Related to this, the heavier passages occur where two or more parts play simultaneously or where the samples consist of multiple sounds, are predominantly low in register or both.

Differences between the Routines of the DMU Crew Compared to those of the Scratch Perverts and The Mixologists

On listening to the three routines, it is evident that while the routines of The Scratch Perverts and The Mixologists have much in common aesthetically, that of the DMU Crew seems different. The DMU Crew routine, for example, consists of only three sections over 11 minutes and 12 seconds, compared to The Mixologists' six sections over 5 minutes and 42 seconds and The Scratch Perverts' six sections over 6 minutes and 11 seconds. However, the length of both The Mixologists' and The Scratch Perverts' routines are fixed, as to showcase their skills at the DMC World Championships their routines cannot exceed 6 minutes in length. The DMU Crew routine is not affected by such a restriction and so to highlight length of their routine, as a great difference is not relevant. What is relevant however, is that during this time the DMU Crew use only half the number of samples of the other two teams over this greater duration making the routine sound much more drawn-out. Although the routine sounds different, the compositional processes used by the DMU Crew are consistent with those of the other two teams. As has been shown in the analysis, the team uses similar samples from the same sample types as the other two teams and uses the same techniques to manipulate those samples – mostly mixing and punchphasing, but also backspinning, scratching and sticker-looping. I believe that the different sound of the DMU Crew is not due to great aesthetic differences but because the team is early in their formation and does not have as much team experience and shared technical proficiency as The Mixologists and The Scratch Perverts. DMU Crew team members, for example, do not tend to share techniques and samples are used at length. This results in the sections having a predominantly layered structure which, while it is also used by The Scratch Perverts, is primarily a characteristic of the DMU Crew. The DMU Crew's use of the layering technique at the exclusion of all others gives their routine a very different quality to that of the other teams and results in textures changing little throughout the sections. What I hope I have shown is that, although the DMU Crew routine has some aesthetic differences with those of the other two teams, these are due, in part, to the different level of experience of the team and not an inconsistency with the genre as established by the other two teams as a whole.

Chapter 10
Conclusion

Over the last 30 years, hip-hop has become recognised as an increasingly influential popular culture. However, despite the credence given to hip-hop culture as being culturally and sociologically important, hip-hop music is rarely taken seriously as an artistic genre. But armed only with turntables, a mixer and a pile of records, hip-hop DJs and turntable musicians, both individually and in groups, have developed innovative techniques and processes that have changed the face of not only how music sounds, but also how it is made.

The aesthetic goals of hip-hop artists have, until recently, been largely excluded from academic work, but hip-hop music is worthy of musicological attention. As well as focusing on the music itself, this study hopes to have provided a new two-stranded framework that allows other people interested in hip-hop turntable music to study not only the musical product, but also the creative process through which it was created, combining process-based analysis with a more formal musicological analysis routine.

Creative collaboration seems inherent to hip-hop, b-boying/b-girling and graffiti both making collective work in similar ways to turntable teams. Hip-hop is characterised by ideas of community and collaboration that, when applied to the creation of hip-hop artefacts, are part of the hip-hop aesthetic.

The turntable has been used as a creative instrument since the early twentieth century, and historical overviews show parallel histories across experimental and popular music. Ideas around the selection and use of the technologies, the reasons behind turntable experimentation and the development of sound manipulation techniques cross these two histories, providing a fluid and vibrant background to hip-hop turntablism.

In the course of this book, a dual-focused analytical methodology for hip-hop turntable music has been developed. The analytical model deals with process as well as the creative product, facilitating and supporting a process-based analysis while also offering a more formal analysis of the routine to establish any characteristics. The analytical framework presents an approach to the analysis of the music of hip-hop turntable teams that deals with elements directly central to turntablism, such as choice and use of sample types and the use of sound manipulation techniques. It is in this area of developing a new analytical methodology specifically for hip-hop turntable music that this approach may be most useful for scholars as it moves away from regarding hip-hop music as an area for primarily sociological or textual study and towards valuing hip-hop music as worthy of study as music itself. A new notation system for turntable music facilitates this process, encompassing material, manipulation techniques and structure, tempo, timescale and the roles of individual musicians. Hopefully, this system will offer a way of notating that can assist the study and analysis of hip-hop turntable music.

Through an analysis of the music and how it is made, the book has shown a number of characteristics of the creative process and musical product of team turntable composition. Fundamental to these is that the turntable is used as a productive musical instrument in both the creation and performance of routines, all of the turntable teams studied creating original music by manipulating isolated parts of existing records. In the creation of these original routines, the hip-hop turntable teams make a collaborative circle. This is formed through friendships and acquaintances and a desire to share common interests, goals, ideas and skills that results in the creation of a collective work. The creation of this collective work involves a high level of collaboration and the creative processes used by all teams demonstrate the existence of devising processes. The teams work within the same five-stage devising framework but details within each phase differ from team to team. Methods of generating and sharing ideas vary, creative frameworks and structures are established differently and reflection and evaluation takes place in different ways. The teams' creation and use of such a flexible framework means that each team is able to work in a way best suited to the team and the individuals within it, customising their own compositional process. It is important to remember, however, that although the teams clearly demonstrate the use of collaboration and devising as central to their creative process, the framework itself is used unconsciously, as the natural process through which to achieve the desired artistic product.

The creation of a model for the devising framework allowed an analysis of the compositional processes of all three teams in the creation of their routines. All three teams studied compose using a similar devising process, regardless of their ability or status. This demonstrates that devising is consistently used as a compositional process in all areas of the hip-hop turntable community, ranging from amateur teams early in their formation to experienced professional teams at the height of their careers. Such a flexible devising process can accommodate different levels of ability and status because central to this process is the creative input and interaction of individual team members who are able to input at their own level. This even allows for teams consisting of members of different ability levels to function positively.

The routines created through this devising process do not require any improvisation during performance and are strictly structured and rehearsed. They have general characteristics with specific differences from team to team. All three routines consist of a number of smaller sections, usually in 4/4 time, though tempos may alter in and between sections. The teams use a wide range of sample types. These are manipulated using a range of techniques that differ in frequency and manner of use from team to team. All teams reflect new sounds and techniques. Roles and responsibilities for particular manipulation techniques are shared between team members. The routines exhibit four main relationships between individual parts, and each team combines these in different ways. Some sample types, manipulation techniques and relationships between parts are specific to a particular team. The teams use similar creative processes and within these processes use the same sample types and manipulation techniques. However, because of the different inputs of the individual members, each routine is different, reflecting the different styles and influences of each member and the team as a whole.

This study of the compositional processes of turntable teams working within hip-hop culture has suggested certain areas of interest, which, although beyond the scope of this book, would be valuable to pursue further. For example, this book focused specifically on the routines of hip-hop turntable teams based in the UK. It would have been interesting to see if the conclusions might be matched by teams based in other countries or whether the collaborative processes exhibited by the teams studied are particular to those working in the UK. Wider reading suggests that the processes evident in the teams based in the UK are matched by those based in the US, but a more thorough exploration would be useful.

This book has had at its heart the *music* of hip-hop turntablism, rather than the celebrities and culture, technologies and techniques more often written about. Focusing on a variety of subjects – from the history of turntable experimentation and the development of innovative sound manipulation techniques, to turntable team formation, collective creation and an analysis of team routines – it has shown how turntable teams have developed new ways of composing music, including innovative sound manipulation techniques and collaborative systems of composition. The innovative and groundbreaking work of hip-hop turntablists has not just influenced the world of hip-hop and wider popular culture, it has changed the world of music as a whole. For over a century, analogue turntables and mixers have been the technologies of choice, but with developments in new digital technologies and the potential creative opportunities these offer, where will turntablism progress next?

Bibliography

A-Trak. Presentation given to Skratchcon 2000, San Francisco, California, 1 July 2000 [Online, 2000]. Available from scratchcon.com [accessed 20 September 2000].

A-Trak. 'Sound Check with DJ A-Trak' [Online, 2008]. Available from www.youtube.com/user/SeratoHQ#p/search/2/gduSsP7b0t0 [accessed 10 February 2012].

Acyde. 'Cuts, Bruises, Turntables and the Whole Truth … The Scratch Perverts' [Online]. *Spine Magazine*. Available from www.spinemagazine.com/features/music/scratchperverts.html [accessed 6 April 2004].

Adorno, T.W. 'The Form of the Record' (1934) in Block, U. and Glasmeier, M. (eds) *Broken Music: Artists' Recordworks* (DAAD, 1989).

Allen, J. *'He's the DJ, I'm the Turntablist': The Progressive Art of Hip Hop DJs* (Mississinewa Press, 1997).

artshole.co.uk. 'White Cube – Christian Marclay' [Online]. Available from www.artshole.co.uk/exhibitions/inside%20white%20cube%20Christian%20Marclay.htm [accessed 16 April 2005].

Baudelaire, C. and Mayne, J. (eds) *The Painter of Modern Life and Other Essays* (Phaidon Press, 1995 [1863]).

Belbin, R.M. *Managerial Teams* (Heinemann, 1981).

Belbin, R.M. *Team Roles at Work* (Butterworth-Heinemann, 1993).

Beni G. Interview with the BBC [Online, 2001]. London, 22 September 2001. Available from www.bbc.co.uk/music/features/vinyl/tbenny.shtml [accessed 28 March 2004].

Beni G. Interview with the author (London, 1 February 2002).

Beni G. Interview with the author (London, 4 April 2003).

Benjamin, W. *Illuminations*, trans. Harry Zohn (Pimlico, 1992).

Block, U. and Glasmeier, M. (eds) *Broken Music: artists' recordworks* (DAAD, 1989).

Bracewell, M. *England is Mine* (Flamingo, 1998).

Brackett, D. 'Where's It At: Postmodern Theory and the Contemporary Musical Field' in Lochhead, J. and Auner, J. *Postmodern Music/Postmodern Thought* (Routledge, 2002).

Bradbury, M. and McFarlane, J. (eds) *Modernism: A Guide to European Literature 1890–1930* (Penguin Books, 1990).

Bray, T. and Middleton, R. 'The Meaning of Modernism' in *The Rise of Modernism in Music 1890–1935*, Unit 32 (The Open University, 1979).

Brewster, B. and Broughton, F. *Ministry of Sound: The Manual* (Headline Book Publishing, 1998).

Brewster, B. and Broughton, F. *Last Night a DJ Saved My Life* (Headline Book Publishing, 1999).

Brewster, B. and Broughton, F. *How to DJ (properly)* (Bantam Press, 2002).

Brooker, P. *Cultural Theory: A Glossary* (Arnold Publishers, 1999).

Bruno, F. 'The DJ's new lexicon' [Online]. *Feed Magazine*. Available from www. feedmag.com [accessed 11 July 2001].

Cage, J. 'The Future of Music: Credo' in Cage, J. *Silence* (Wesleyan University Press, 1937).

Cage, J. 'For More New Sounds' in Kostelanetz, R. (ed.) *John Cage: An Anthology* (Da Capo Press, 1970).

Cage, J. *Silence* (Wesleyan University Press, 1973).

Cage, J. and Hoover, K. *Virgil Thomson: His Life and Music* (T. Yoseloff, 1959).

Calinescu, M. *Five Faces for Modernity* (Duke University Press, 1987).

Carluccio, J., Imboden, E. and Pirtle, R. 'Turntable Transcription Methodology' [Online, 2000]. Available from www.battlesounds.com [accessed 20 November 2000].

Chadabe, J. *Electric Sound: The Past and Promise of Electronic Music* (Prentice Hall, 1997).

Chambers, I. *Popular Culture: The Metropolitan Experience* (Methuen & Co, 1986).

Chang, J. *Can't Stop Won't Stop, a History of the Hip-Hop Generation* (St Martin's Press, 2005).

Chang, J. (ed.) *Total Chaos: The Art and Aesthetics of Hip-Hop* (Basic Civitas Books, 2007).

Chester, A. 'Second Thoughts on a Rock Aesthetic: The Band' in Frith, S. and Goodwin, A. *On Record* (Routledge, 2000).

Chew, V.K. *Talking Machines* (Her Majesty's Stationary Office, 1967).

Christen, R.S. 'Hip Hop Learning: Graffiti as an Educator of Urban Teenagers'. *Educational Foundations Journal*, Fall 2003.

Coleman, M. *Playback* (Da Capo Press, 2003).

Collins, N. (ed.) 'Groove, Pit and Wave: Recording, Transmission and Music'. *Leonardo Music Journal*, Vol. 13 (2003).

Couper, M. (ed.) *New Oxford History of Music Volume X: The Modern Age 1860–1960* (Oxford University Press, 1975).

Cox, C. (ed.) 'Clubbers Guide to DJing'. *Ministry of Sound Magazine* (1998).

Cutler, C. 'Technology, politics and contemporary music: Necessity and choice in musical forms' in Middleton, R. (ed.) *Popular Music 4: Performers and Audiences* (Cambridge University Press, 1984).

Dammert, H. 'Grammophon-Konzerte' in *Musikblatter des Anbruch 8*, October-November (1926), 406–7.

Denis, R. 'Twenty-five Old School Turning Points' in *The Source*, November (1993).

Dimitriadis, G. *Performing Identity/Performing Culture* (Peter Lang Publishing, 2001).

Dimitriadis, G. 'Hip-Hop: From Live Performance to Mediated Narrative' in Forman, M. and Neal, M.A. (eds) *That's the Joint! The Hip-Hop Studies Reader* (Routledge, 2007), 421–34.

DJ Hooch. *B-Boy Championships: From Bronx to Brixton* (Random House, 2011).

DJ Maurice Norris. 'Is Digital DJing Killing the Art' [Online, 2011]. Available from digitaldjtools.net/articles/is-digital-djing-killing-the-art/ [accessed 2 February 2012].

DJ Rocc. 'The Beat Junkies in the Studio with Serato' [Online, 2011]. Available from www.youtube.com/user/SeratoHQ#p/search/0/288JQ7qtWT4 [accessed 2 March 2011]

DJ Shiftee. 'Shiftee's Tutorial for Breakfast of Champions' [Online, 2011]. Available from www.native-instruments.com/#/en/products/dj/traktor-scratch-pro-2/?content=1564&page=2058 [accessed 3 February 2012).

djstore.com. 'Digital Vinyl Systems (DVS)' [Online, 2012]. Available from www.djstore.com/html/guideDVS.php [accessed 23 February 2012].

dmcworlddjchamps. 'The DMC World DJ Championships Rules' [Online, 2011]. Available from www.dmcdjchamps.com/rules.php [accessed on 23 February 2012].

DMU Crew. Transcription of rehearsal process by the author (Leicester, May 2002).

DMU Crew. Interview with the author (Leicester, May 2003).

Doc Rice. 'Proposal for notation system of turntable music, draft three' [Online, 1998]. Available from www.wicked-styles.com [accessed 2 April 2001].

Docuyanan, F. 'Governing Graffiti in Contested Urban Spaces' in *PoLAR: Political and Legal Anthropology Review*, 23 (2000), 103–21.

Duro, P. and Greenhalgh, M. *Essential Art History* (Bloomsbury, 1993).

Edgar, A. and Sedwick, P. *Key Concepts in Cultural Theory* (Routledge, 1999).

efnx.com. 'Concerto for Turntable' [Online, 2001]. Available from www.efnx.com/old/turntableproject/Concerto%20For%20Turntable.pdf [accessed 26 February 2012].

Emsley, J. *The Laptop DJ Handbook* (Course Technology PTR, 2011).

Endelman, M. 'Scratching without vinyl: A hip-hop revolution' [Online, 2002]. Available from http://query.nytimes.com/gst/fullpage.html?res=9500E0DD1F38F930A35751C1A9649C8B63 [accessed 6 October 2007].

Farrell, M. *Collaborative Circles* (The University of Chicago Press, 2001).

Farrer, P. 'DJ2000, Professional DJ Mixer', review in *Sound on Sound*, September 1998.

Felipe 'Interview with Beni G' [Online, 2001]. Available from www.djbattle.net/intervjuer.php?articleID=955&page=1 [accessed 6 April 2004].

Fernando, S.H. *The New Beats, Exploring the Music, Culture and Attitudes of Hip-Hop* (Payback Press, 1995).

FLOWREXsac. Response to forum post from author [Online, 2012]. Available from www.ukbboy.info/forum/topic/16035-input-into-book-crew-routines [accessed 23 February 2012].

Forman, M. and Neal, M.A. (eds) *That's the Joint! The Hip-Hop Studies Reader* (Routledge, 2004).

Foster, H. *The Return of the Real: The Avant-Garde at the End of the Century* (MIT Press, 1996).

Friere, S. 'Early Musical Impressions from Both Sides of the Loudspeaker'. *Leonardo Music Journal*, Vol. 133 (2003), 67–71.

Frith, S. *Performing Rites: On the Value of Popular Music* (Oxford University Press, 1996).

Frith, S. and Goodwin, A. *On Record: Rock, Pop and the Written Word* (Routledge, 2000).

Frith, S., Straw, W. and Street, J (eds) *The Cambridge Companion to Pop and Rock* (Cambridge University Press, 2001).

Garratt, S. *Adventures in Wonderland* (Headline Book Publishing, 1998).

Gaunt, K.D. 'The veneration of James Brown and George Clinton in hip-hop music: Is it live! Or is it memory?' *Popular Music: Style and Identity* (Centre for Research on Canadian Cultural Industries and Institutions, 1995).

Gee, B. 'The Mixologists deliver their cargo' [Online]. Available from www.splinterdata.com/?bulletin=9&bbite=129 [accessed 6 April 2004].

Gilson, E. *Introduction aux arts du beau* (Paris, 1963).

Glasmeier, M. 'Music of the Angels' in Block, U. and Glasmeier, M. (eds) *Broken Music: Artists' Recordworks* (DAAD, 1989).

Goffman, E. *The Presentation of Self in Everyday Life* (Penguin, 1971).

Goodall, H. *Big Bangs* (Vintage, 2001).

Goodwin, A. 'Popular music and postmodern theory'. *The Postmodern Arts – An Introductory Reader* (Routledge, 1995).

Gragg, R. 'Turntablists are the true visionaries [Online, 1999]. Available from www.ncra.ca/business/turntablism/ttarticles.html [accessed 20 June 2005].

Griffiths, P. *A Guide to Electronic Music* (Thames and Hudson, 1979).

Griffiths, P. *Modern Music and After* (Oxford University Press, 1995).

Griffiths, P. *Dictionary of Twentieth Century Music* (Thames and Hudson, 1996).

Gross, J. 'Christian Marclay' [Online, 1998]. Available from www.furious.com/perfect/christianmarclay.html [accessed 26 October 2012].

Harrison, C. *Modern Art and Modernism, Introduction: Modernism, Problems and Methods* (Open University Press, 1983).

Harrison, C. *Essays on Art and Language* (Basil Blackwell, 1991).

Harrison, C. and Orton, F. (eds) *Modernism, Criticism, Realism* (Harper and Row, 1994).

Harvey, D. *The Condition of Postmodernity* (Basil Blackwell, 1989).

Hawkins, S. *Settling the Pop Score: Pop Texts and Identity Politics* (Ashgate, 2002).

Hayward, P. *Culture, Technology and Creativity in the Late Twentieth Century* (University of Luton Press, 1990).

Hoch, D. 'Toward a Hip-Hop Aesthetic' in Chang, J. (ed.) *Total Chaos: The Art and Aesthetics of Hip-Hop* (Basic Civitas Books, 2007), 349–64.

Hosokawa, S. *The Aesthetics of Recorded Sound* (English Summary, 1990).

Huyssen, A. *After the Great Divide* (Macmillan, 1986).

J.P. 'Exclusive interview with The Scratch Perverts on DJ, turntablist and hip hop culture' [Online, 2003]. Available from http://www.turntablink.com/latest/interview01.htm [accessed 6 April 2004].

Jazzy Jeff. 'Jazzy Jeff on Serato' [Online, 2006]. Available from www.youtube.com/watch?v=VR8McH5pe64 [accessed 12 October 2007].

Kahn, D. 'Christian Marclay's Early Years: An Interview'. *Leonardo Music Journal*, Vol. 13 (2003), 17–21.

Katz, M. *Capturing Sound* (University of California Press, 2005).

Keller, H. 'Rap' in *Sounds*, November (1981).

Kempster, C. (ed.) *History of House* (Sanctuary Publishing, 1996).

Keyes, C. 'At the Crossroads: Rap music and its African nexus'. *Ethnomusicology*, Vol. 40, No. 2 (1996), 223–48.

Kjølner, T. *A Handbook for Devising* [Online, 2001]. Available from http://devised.hku.nl [accessed 3 November 2003].

Kogun. 'Interview with Radar' [Online, 2001]. Available from www.rawskills.com [accessed 15 May 2001].

Kostelanetz, R. (ed.) *John Cage: An Anthology* (Da Capo Press, 1991 [1970]).

KRS-ONE. *Ruminations* (Front Page Entertainment, 2003).

Kramer, J. 'The Nature and Origins of Musical Postmodernism' in Lochhead, J. and Auner, J. *Postmodern Music/Postmodern Thought* (Routledge, 2002).

Krims, A. *Rap Music and the Poetics of Identity* (Cambridge University Press, 2000).

Lamden, G. *Devising* (Hodder and Stoughton, 2000).

Landy, L. and Jamieson, E. *Devising Dance and Music: idée fixe: Experimental Sound and Movement Theatre* (University of Sunderland Press, 2000).

Lebrecht, N. *The Companion to Twentieth Century Music* (Simon and Schuster Ltd, 1992).

Lippit, T.M. 'Turntable Music in the Digital Era: Designing Alternative Tools for New Turntable Expression'. *Proceedings of the 2006 International Conference on New Interfaces for Musical Expression* (NIME06) Paris, France (2006).

Lochhead, J. and Auner, J. *Postmodern Music/Postmodern Thought* (Routledge, 2002).

Lothar, R. *Die Sprechmaschine. Ein technisch-aesthetischer Versuch* (Leipzig, 1942).

McClary, S. and Walser, R. 'Start Making Sense! Musicology Wrestles with Rock' in Frith, S. and Goodwin, A. *On Record* (Routledge, 2000).

McGuigan, J. *Modernity and Postmodern Culture* (Open University Press, 1999).

McHard, J. *The Future of Modern Music* (American Book Publishing, 2001).

McHard, J. 'The State of Modern Music' [Online]. Available from www.future ofmodernmusic.com/article-1.html [accessed 16 April 2005].

McRobbie, A. *Postmodernism and Popular Culture* (Routledge, 1994).

Maffesoli, M. *El Tiempo de Las Tribus. El Declive Del Individualismo en Las Sociedades de Masa* (Icaria, 1990).

MajikFist. 'Talking with the Perverts' [Online, 2004]. Available from www.4clubbers. net/interviews/scratchperverts.htm [accessed 6 April 2004].

Manning, P. 'The Influence of Recording Technologies on the Early Development of Electroacoustic Music'. *Leonardo Music Journal*, Vol. 13 (2003), 5–10.

Marcus, L. 'Scratch Perverts: Primed for Action' [Online]. Available from www. xpressmag.com.au/salt/coverstory/784scratchperverts.htm [accessed 6 April 2004].

Masterfaders. 'DJing tips' [Online]. Available from www.rawskills.com [accessed 15 May 2001].

Meyer, L.B. *Music, the Arts and Ideas* (University of Chicago Press, 1967).

Middleton, R. (ed.) *Reading Pop: Approaches to Textual Analysis in Popular Music* (Oxford University Press, 2000a).

Middleton, R. 'Popular Music Analysis and Musicology: Bridging the Gap' in Middleton, R. (ed.) *Reading Pop: Approaches to Textual Analysis in Popular Music* (Oxford University Press, 2000b).

Middleton, R. 'Pop, rock and interpretation' in Frith, S., Straw, W. and Street, J. (eds) *The Cambridge Companion to Pop and Rock* (Cambridge University Press, 2001).

Miller, P. *Rhythm Science* (Mediawork/The MIT Press, 2004).

Miller, S. *The Last Post: Music after Modernism* (Manchester University Press, 1993).

Moholy-Nagy, L. 'Produktion-Reprodukion'. *De Stijl*, no. 7, translated in *Maholy_ Nagy*, Krisztina Passuth (ed. and trans.) (Thames and Hudson, 1923), 290.

Moholy-Nagy, L. 'Neue Gestaltung in der Musik, Moglichkeiten des Grammophons'. *Der Sturm*, 7 (1923), translated in Block, U. and Glasmeier, M. (eds) *Broken Music: Artists' Recordworks* (DAAD, 1989).

Molino, J. 'Esquisse d'une semiologie de la poesie'. *La petite revue de philosophie*, Vol. 6, No. 1 (1984), 1–36.

Montano, E. '"How do you know he's not playing Pac-Man while he's supposed to be DJing?": Technology, formats and the digital future of DJ culture'. *Popular Music*, Vol. 29, No. 3 (2010), 397–416.

Moore, A.F. *Rock: The Primary Text: Developing a Musicology of Rock* (Ashgate, 2001).

Morgan, R.P. *Modern Times – From World War One to the Present* (Macmillan, 1993).

Native Instruments. 'Turntablist legend DJ Craze Performs on Traktor Scratch Pro and Kontrol X1' [Online, 12 May 2010]. Native Instruments' You Tube Channel. Available from http://www.youtube.com/watch?v=aCA4yiPfFIg [accessed 26 October 2012].

Native Instruments. 'DJ Craze performs on the new Traktor Scratch Pro 2' [Online, 30 March 2011]. Native Instruments' You Tube Channel. Available from http://www.youtube.com/watch?v=msdFDCcdwaA [accessed 26 October 2012].

Nativeinstruments.com. 'Introduction: New Traktor Scratch Systems' [Online, 2012]. Available from www.native-instruments.com/#/en/products/dj/traktor-scratch-pro-2/?content=1502&page=2059 [accessed 2 February 2012].

Nattiez, J.J. *Music and Discourse: Toward a Semiology of Music* (Princeton University Press, 1990).

Neale, S. 'A question of genre'. *Screen*, Vol. 31, No. 1 (1990).

Newman, M. 'History of Turntablism' [Online, 2002]. Available from www.pedestrian.info/PedestrianHistoryofTurntablism.pdf [accessed 12 April 2004].

Nicholls, P. *Modernisms: A Literary Guide* (Macmillan, 1995).

Nova, C. 'Mr Thing' [Online, 2002]. Available from www.residentadvisor.net/feature view.asp?id=190 [accessed 6 April 2004].

Oddey, A. *Devising Theatre* (Routledge Press, 1994).

Ord-Hume, A.W.J.G. *Clockwork Music* (George Allen and Unwin Ltd, 1973).

Paddison, M. *Adorno, Modernism and Mass Culture* (Kahn & Averill, 1996).

Pape, G. 'Foreword to *The Future of Modern Music*' [Online]. Available from www.thefutureofmodernmusic.com/book%20excerpts%20-%20foreword.htm [accessed 16 April 2005].

Pemberton, D. 'Scratch 'n' riff DJs turn the tables on rock'. *The Daily Express* (23 April 1998).

Piper Clendinning, J. 'Postmodern Architecture/Postmodern Music' in Lochhead, J. and Auner, J. *Postmodern Music/Postmodern Thought* (Routledge, 2002).

Plus One. Interview with the BBC [Online]. Available from www.bbc.co.uk/music/features/vinyl/tpluone.shtml [accessed 28 March 2004].

Poschardt, U. *DJ Culture* (Quartet Books, 1998).

Potter, R.A. *Spectacular Vernaculars: Hip Hop and the Politics of Postmodernism* (State University of New York Press, 1995).

Price, E.G. *Hip Hop Culture* (ABC-CLIO, 2006).

Prime Cuts, in Cox, C. (ed.) 'Clubbers Guide to DJing'. *Ministry of Sound*.

Radar. Presentation given to Skratchcon 2000, San Francisco, California, 1 July 2000 [Online]. Available from scratchcon.com [accessed 20 September 2000].

Rahn, J. *Painting Without Permission* (Bergin and Garvey, 2002).

Ratz, S. 'DJ Radar interview' [Online, 2001]. Available from www.discjockey101.com [accessed 15 May 2001].

rawskills.com. 'Mastersfaders' Scratch Notation' [Online]. Available from www.rawskills.com/masterfaders [accessed 14 March 2003].

Reighley, K. *Looking for the Perfect Beat – The Art and Culture of the DJ* (MTV Books/Pocket Books 2000).

Residentadvisor.com. 'Panasonic confirms the end of Technics turntable' [Online, 2010]. Available from www.residentadvisor.net/news.aspx?id=13154 [accessed 3 February 2012].

Reynolds, S. *Energy Flash* (Picador, 1998).

Rollinson, D., Broadfield, A. and Edwards, D. *Organisational Behaviour and Analysis: An Integrated Approach* (Addison-Wesley, 1998).

Rose, T. *Black Noise* (Wesleyan University Press, 1994).

Schaeffer, P. *A La Recherche d'une Musique Concrète* (Le Seuil, 1952).

Schaeffer, P. 'Esquisse d'un Solfège Concret' in Schaeffer, P. *A La Recherche d'une Musique Concrète* (Le Seuil, 1952).

Schein, E.H. *Organisational Psychology* (Prentice Hall, 1980).

Schloss, J.G. *Making Beats: The Art of Sample-Based Hip-Hop* (Wesleyan University Press, 2004).

Schloss, J. 'The Art of Battling: An Interview with Zulu King Alien Ness' in Chang, J. (ed.) *Total Chaos: The Art and Aesthetics of Hip-Hop* (Basic Civitas Books, 2007), 27–32

Schloss, J.G. *Foundation* (Oxford University Press, 2009).

Scratch Perverts. Presentation given to Skratchcon 2000, San Francisco, California, 1 July 2000 [Online]. Available from scratchcon.com [accessed 20 September 2000].

Settle, M. 'Oh wait ... DMC is going digital after all' [Online, 2010]. Available from www.skratchworx.com/newspage.php4?p=archive&fn_mode=comments &fn_id=1562 [accessed 3 February 2012].

Shapiro, P. 'Reinventing the Wheels of Steel'. *The Wire*, June (1997), 8–24.

Shapiro, P. 'Mixed Medium'. *The Wire*, March (1998), 16.

Shapiro, P. 'The Primer'. *The Wire*, January (1999), 40–45.

Shuker, R. *Understanding Popular Music* (Routledge, 2003).

Stoner, J.A.F. 'Risky and cautious shifts in group decisions: The influence of widely held values'. *Journal of Experimental Social Psychology*, Vol. 4, No. 2 (1961), 442–59.

Storey, J. *An Introduction to Cultural Theory and Popular Culture* (Prentice Hall, 1993).

Strinati, D. *An Introduction to Theories of Popular Culture* (Routledge, 1995).

Stuckenschmidt, H.H. 'Machines – A Vision for the Future'. *Modern Music*, 4, March-April (1927), 8–14.

Shuker, R. *Understanding Popular Music* (Taylor and Francis, 2001).

Shuker, R. *Key Concepts in Popular Music* (Routledge, 2002).

Tagg, P. 'Fernando the Flute', Unpublished conference paper (University of Liverpool, 1991).

Tagg, P. 'Analysing Popular Music: Theory, Method and Practice' in Middleton, R. (ed.) *Reading Pop* (Oxford University Press, 2000).

Taylor, P. *Impresario: Malcolm McLaren and the British New Wave* (MIT Publishing, 1998).

Taylor, T. 'Music and Musical Practices in Postmodernity' in Lochhead, J. and Auner, J. *Postmodern Music/Postmodern Thought* (Routledge, 2002).

Theberge, P. 'Random access: Music, technology, postmodernism' in Miller, S. *The Last Post* (Manchester University Press, 1993).

Thornton, S. *Club Cultures* (Polity Press, 1995).

Toch, E. 'Uber meine Kantate "Das Wasser" und meine Grammophonmusik'. *Melos*, 9, May-June (1930), 221–2.

Toop, D. *Ocean of Sound* (Serpent's Tail, 1995).

Toop, D. *Rap Attack 3* (Serpent's Tail, 2000).

Toop, D. 'Uptown Throwdown' in Forman, M. and Neal, M.A. (eds) *That's the Joint! The Hip-Hop Studies Reader* (Routledge, 2004).

Tuckmann, B.W. 'Development sequence in small groups'. *Psychological Bulletin*, Vol. 63, No. 3 (1965), 384–99.

Tuckmann, B.W. and Jenson, N. 'Stages of group development revisited'. *Group and Organisation Studies*, Vol. 2, No. 3 (1977), 419–27.

ukhh.com. 'Scratch Perverts: Profile' [Online]. Available from www.ukhh.com/bhhartists/scratch_perverts_profile.htm [accessed 6 April 2004].

United DJs. 'Interview with DJ Plus One' [Online]. Available from www.djsunited.com.au/plusone.html [accessed 6 April 2004].

Valle, I. and Weiss, E. 'Participation in the figured world of graffiti'. *Teaching and Teacher Education*, Vol. 26 (2010), 128–35.

Vegas, T. Interview with the BBC [Online]. Available from www.bbc.co.uk/music/features/vinyl/ttonyvegas.shtml [accessed 28 March 2004].

Vode, Z. 'The Evolution of a Disc Jockey in the Hip-Hop Culture' [Online, 2000]. Available from www.turntablism.com [accessed 7 April 2000].

Wenger, E. 'Communities of practice, a brief introduction' [Online, 2008]. Available from www.ewenger.com/theory/index.htm [accessed on 23 February 2012].

Wall, T. *Studying Popular Music Culture* (Arnold, 2003).

Walser, R. 'Rhythm, rhyme and rhetoric in the music of Public Enemy'. *Ethnomusicology*, Vol. 39, No. 2 (1995), 193–218.

Wang, O. 'Higher Science'. *LA Weekly*, 25–31 August 2000. Available from www.laweekly.com [accessed 2 April 2001].

Wax Factor. 'Prime Cuts' [Online, 1999]. The Vinyl Exchange. Available from www.vinylexchange.com/backishez/primecutsback.html [accessed 6 April 2004].

Webber, S. *Turntable Technique: The Art of the DJ* (Berklee Press, 2000).

Wheale, N. *The Postmodern Arts – An Introductory Reader* (Routledge, 1995).

White, M. *The World the Music Made: Hip Hop and Its Milieu.* Master's thesis (University of Washington, 1996).

White, M. 'The Phonograph Turntable and Performance Practice in Hip Hop Music' [Online]. Ethnomusicology Online. Available from www.research.umbc.edu/eol/2/white/html [accessed 28 March 2004].

Wildstyle Network. 'The Mixologists – U.K.'s Innovative DJ Stylers' [Online]. Available from www.wildstylenetwork.com/justurban/artists/DJs/MIXOLOGISTS/infoen.htm [accessed 6 April 2004].

Willis, P. *Moving Culture* (Calouste Gulbenkian Foundation, 1990).

Wimsatt, W.U. *Bomb the Suburbs* (Soft Skull Press, 2000).

Youtube. 'Turntablist legend DJ Craze Performs on Traktor Scratch Pro and Kontrol X1' [Online, 2010]. Available from www.youtube.com/watch?v=aCA4yiPfFIg [accessed 2 February 2012].

Youtube. 'DJ Craze performs on the new Traktor Scratch Pro 2' [Online, 2011]. Available from http://www.youtube.com/watch?v=msdFDCcdwaA [accessed 23 February 2012].

Zaid. 'The Mixologists' [Online]. The Vinyl Exchange. Available from www. vinylexchange.com/mixologists.html [accessed 31 Dec 2001].

Zeller, H.R. 'Media Composition According to Cage' in Block, U. and Glasmeier, M. (eds) *Broken Music: Artists' Recordworks* (DAAD, 1989).

Discography

Bambaataa, Afrika. (1986) Planet Rock, *Planet Rock – The Album.* Tommy Boy Records TBLP1007.

Cage, John. (1996 [1939]) Imaginary Landscape No. 1. *Imaginary Landscapes.* Hat Art CD6179.

Cage, John. (2001 [1942]) Credo in Us, *Credo in Us – More Works for Percussion.* Wergo WER 6651–2.

Cage, John. (1996 [1943]) Imaginary Landscape No. 3. *Imaginary Landscapes.* Hat Art CD6179.

Cage, John. (1996 [1952]) Imaginary Landscape No. 5. *Imaginary Landscapes.* Hat Art CD6179.

Cage, John. (2004 [1960]) *Cartridge Music.* Edition Wandelweiser Records 0406.

Cage, John (2012 [1969] [Online]. Available from http://archive.org/details/ C_1969_11_21_2 [accessed 26 October 2012].

Hancock, Herbie. (1999) Rockit, *Future Shock.* Columbia CK 65962.

Marclay, Christian. (1990) *Footsteps.* RecRec Music, RecRecLP26.

Marclay, Christian. (2003) John Cage, *More Encores.* 3EFA 12676.

Schaeffer, Pierre. (1999 [1948]) Etude aux Chemin de Fer, *L'Ouevre Musicale.* Musidisc INA292572.

Schaeffer, Pierre. (1999 [1948]) Etude Pathetique, *L'Ouevre Musicale,* Musidisc INA292572

Schaeffer, Pierre. (1999 [1948]) Etude aux Tourniquets, *L'Ouevre Musicale.* Musidisc INA292572.

Schaeffer, Pierre. (1999 [1948]) Etude Violette, *L'Ouevre Musicale.* Musidisc INA292572.

Thomson, Virgil. (2000 [1926–8]) Symphony on a Hymn Tune, *Symphony No 1–3.* Naxos 8.559022.

Videography

A Vestax Master-Class (1998). Vestax, Europe. 28min [Video: VHS].

DMC 1999 DJ Team Championship. (1999) DMC, London. 96min [Video: VHS].

DMC 2000 World Team Championship. (2000) DMC, London. 90min [Video: VHS].

DMC 2001 World Team Championship. (2001) DMC, London. 91min [Video: VHS].

DMC 2002 World Team Championship. (2002) DMC, London [Video: VHS].

Scratch. (2002) Directed by Doug Pray, Momentum Pictures, 87min [Video: VHS].

So You Wanna Be a DJ? (1996) DMC, London. 101min [Video: VHS].

Video footage of the DMU Crew process and performance. (2002) Leicester, unpublished [Video: VHS].

Video footage of The Mixologists' performance of routine for DMC Team Championship 2000. Unpublished [Video: VHS].

Video footage of The Mixologists' rehearsal of the routine for the DMC Team Championship 2000. Unpublished [Video: VHS].

Index

Bold page numbers indicate figures, *italic* numbers indicate tables.

A-Trak 39, 40, 90–92, 94, 95
adjourning 52
Adorno, Theodor 17
analytical methodologies
    creative process, need to include in
        72–3
    frameworks for 73–9, *74*, *75*, *76–7*, *78–9*
    limitations of current 71–3
    poetics 72–3
    see also compositional process,
        analysis of; routines, analysis of
Animatronik 12
Antimatter (Radar) 93
Arma, Paul 19, 45
artistic concept, development and reflection
    of 36

b-boying
    community as central to 10–11
    creating routines 11–12
backspinning 44, 114, 126, 135, 141, 142
Bambaata, Afrika 43–4, 45
battle crews
    community as central to 10–11
    creating routines 11–12
    see also compositional process,
        analysis of; DMU Crew;
        Mixologists; routines, analysis of;
        Scratch Perverts
beat juggling 47–8, 135, 141
Beni G 26, 53–4, 56, 59–60, 62, 118, 119,
        121, 126, 127, 128, 139
binary form 143
breakbeat 43–4

Cage, John 18, 21–2, 25, 34, 36
Carluccio, J. 87, **88**, **89**, 90, 95
Chase, Charlie 45

Clock Theory 44
collaboration
    b-boying 10–11, *10–12*
    as central to hip-hop 9
    centrality of in devising 65
    collective creation process 104–12,
        117–22, 129–31, 138–9
    graffiti 12–14
collaborative circles
    collective action 63–4
    creative work 60–63
    defined 52
    formation 53–6
    individual practice 61
    innovation as prime focus of 56–7, 58–9
    negotiation of a new vision 58–60
    rebellion against authority 56–8
    risk taking in 58–9
    role allocation 55–6, 63–4
Collaborative Circles (Farrell) 52
collectiveness
    b-boying 10–11, *10–12*
    as central to hip-hop 9
    collective creation process 104–12,
        117–22, 129–31, 138–9
    graffiti 12–14
    see also collaborative circles
community
    b-boying 10–11, *10–12*
    as central to hip-hop 9
    collective creation process 104–12,
        117–22, 129–31, 138–9
    graffiti 12–14
    see also collaborative circles
competition
    as group ethic 61
    as opportunities 63
    Scratch Perverts 57

compositional process, analysis of
  characteristics of routines 140–45
  characteristics of the process 138–9
  collective creation process 104–12,
    117–22, 129–31
  devising framework 138–9
  DMU Crew routine 103–18, *112, 113*,
    116
  final rehearsals and performance
    111–12, 122, 131
  general properties of routine 112, *112*,
    122–3, *123*, 132, *132*
  group organisation 112, 122, 131
  manipulation techniques 114–15, *116*,
    125–8, *127*, 135–7, *136*
  Mixologists routine 117–28, *123, 124,
    125, 127*
  phase 1 rehearsals 106–8, 120–21,
    130–31
  phase 2 rehearsals 108–11, 121–2,
    130–31
  pre-devising administration 104,
    117–18, 129
  preliminary rehearsals 105–6, 118–20,
    129–30
  roles and responsibilities in groups
    142–3
  sample choice for routine 113, *113*,
    123–4, *124, 133*, 133–4
  Scratch Perverts routine 129–38, *132,
    133, 136*
  structure of routine 113–14, 125, *125*,
    134–5
  texture 116–17, 128, 137–8
  transcription techniques for 94–100,
    96, 97, 98, *99, 100*
consumption and production, turntablism
  as both 27
Crab scratch 47
Craze (DJ) 39
Crazy Legs 10–11
crews, battle
  community as central to 10–11
  creating routines 11–12
  see also compositional process,
    analysis of; DMU Crew;
    Mixologists; routines, analysis of;
    Scratch Perverts

cultural studies of hip-hop music 1–2
Curtis, Bill 22
cutting and pasting 24–5, 46

Dammert, Hansjörg 17
dance, b-boying 10–12
delinquent gangs, collaborative circles as
  56–8
devising
  centrality of collaboration in 65
  model framework for process 70, *70*
  processes, frameworks for 66–70, *70*
  see also compositional process,
    analysis of
digital technology, impact on DJ-ing 37–42
Disc (DJ) 47
diversity of music used 45
DJ-ing
  defined 3
  digital technology, impact of on 37–42
  history of 22–5
  reasons for experimentation 37
DMC World DJ Championships 38
DMU Crew
  characteristics of routines 140–45
  collective action 63
  collective creation process 103–12
  common artistic ground 54–5
  compared to Scratch Perverts/
    Mixologists 145–6
  competitions 63
  compositional process, analysis of
    103–18, *112, 113*, **116**
  creative work 60
  devising framework 138–9
  final rehearsals and performance
    111–12
  formation of 54–5
  general properties of routine 112, *112*
  group organisation 112
  innovation as focus 57
  layering technique 143
  Leicester May 2002 routine 103–18,
    112, 113, **116**
  manipulation techniques 114–15, *116*,
    141–2, *142*
  phase 1 rehearsals 106–8
  phase 2 rehearsals 108–11

pre-devising administration 104
preliminary rehearsals 105–6
reasons for choosing 2
relationships between parts of routine 144
role allocation in 55, 56, 104
sample choice for routine 113, *113*, 140–41
structure of routine 113–14, 143
texture 116–17, 144–5
Doc Rice, notation developed by 84–6, *85*
Dog Paddle 44
D.ST 48
DSTRBO 14

EAZ ONE 13–14
Edison, Thomas 15–16
Emiko 10
equipment. *see* technology
ethnicity, spilt within teams 3
experimental music, history of 18–22
experimentation
    reasons for 35–7
    and turntablism 26–7

First Base 136, 137
Fischinger, Oskar 19, 45
Flare (DJ) 47
flare scratch 47
FLOWREXsac 10, 11, 12
forming 52

gender spilt within teams 3
Gibbons, Walter 24–5, 37
Go (DJ) 53, 56, 126, 127–8
graffiti
    community as central to 12–14
    creating artwork 13–14
    guilds 13
Grainger, Percy 18
gramophones, early experiments with 16–19
Grandmaster Flash 30, 44
graphic notation 87–92, **88, 89**
graphophones 16
Grasso, Francis 22, 23–4, 37
group polarisation 58
groups
    advantages of working in 51–2

common artistic grounds 54–5
organisation of during routines 112, 122, 131
roles in 55–6, 104, 142–3
stages of development 52
see also collaborative circles
guilds, graffiti 13

Herc, Kool 43–4
Hindemith, Paul 18, 19, 33
hip-hop music
    aesthetic elements 14
    emergence of 3–4
    methodology for research 2
    previous studies of 1–2
historical studies of hip-hop music 1–2
history
    cutting and pasting 24–5
    DJ-ing 22–5
    experimental music 18–22
    graphophones 16–18
    mixing 23–4
    modernism/postmodernism 25–8
    phonographs 15–16, 18–19
    physical properties of records 19–20
    rewinding 24
    turntables, manipulation using 20–22
home recordings 15–16

Imboden, E. 87, **88, 89**, 90, 95
innovation
    as prime focus of groups 56–7
    and turntablism 26–7
integration as central to hip-hop 9
    see also collaboration

Jazzy, Jeff (DJ) 42

Kid Koala 49
Knuckles, Frankie 24, 37
KRS-One 9

languages, new musical, development of 35–6
layering technique 143
Levan, Larry 24
Love, Harry 53, 55

manipulation techniques
   analysis of during routines 114–15,
      116, 125–8, *127*, 135–7, *136*, 141–2
   backspinning 44, 114, 125, 126, 141,
      142
   beat juggling 47–8, 135, 141
   breakbeat 43–4
   diversity of music used 45
   DMU Crew 114–15, *116*, 142
   melodic 48–9
   mixing 23–4, 44–5, 114, 126
   Mixologists 125–8, *127*, 142
   physical properties of records 19–20
   pitch alteration 126
   primary/secondary users 115, 126–8,
      135–7, 142
   punchphasing 44, 114, 126, 135, 141–2
   record tapping 126
   rhythmic 45–8
   Scratch Perverts 135–7, *136*, 142–3
   scratching 30, 45–7, 114–15, 126, 135,
      141, 142
   sticker loops 115, 142
   structural 43–5
   turntables, using 20–22
Marclay, Christian 20, 25, 33, 34, 36
Masterfaders Crew 92, 95
MC-ing defined 3
McLaren, Malcolm 3
melodic techniques 48–9
Milhaud, Darius 18–19
mixers 32
mixing 23–4, 44–5, 114, 126
Mixologists, The
   binary form 143
   chain form 143
   characteristics of routines 140–45
   collective action 63
   collective creation process 117–22
   competitions 63
   compositional process, analysis of
      117–28, *123*, *124*, *125*, *127*
   creative work 60
   devising framework 138–9
   DMU Crew compared to 145–6
   final rehearsals and performance 122
   formation of 53
   general properties of routine 122–3, *123*

   innovation as focus 57
   London, Sept 2001 117–27, *123*, *124*,
      125, *127*
   manipulation techniques 125–8, *127*,
      141–2, 142
   negotiation of a new vision 59–60
   phase 1 rehearsals 120–21
   phase 2 rehearsals 121–2
   pre-devising administration 117–18
   preliminary rehearsals 118–20
   questioning label of 'turntablism' 57–8
   reasons for choosing 2
   relationships between parts of routine
      144
   role allocation in 55, 56
   sample choice for routine 123–4, *124*,
      140–41
   structure of routine 143
   texture 128, 144–5
modernism/postmodernism 25–8
Moholy-Nagy, Làzló 19, 25, 32, 33, 35, 45
Molino, J. 72–3
Mr Thing (DJ) 62, 137
musical languages, new, development of
   35–6
musicology, traditional 77

negotiation of a new vision 58–60
Noel, Terry 23, 34
norming 52
Norris, Maurice 38, 40, 41–2
notation techniques
   for analysis of compositions 94–101,
      96, **97**, **98**, *99*, *100*
   functions of 92–4, **93**
   graphic notation 87–92, **88**, **89**
   limitations of for popular music 81–2
   need for standardised form 82
   staff notation 82–7, *85*, **86**, **87**

open-fader scratching 46
Orbit scratch 47

performing 52
Perverted Allies, formation of 54
Phone Dial 44
phonographs 15–16, 18–19
physical properties of records 19–20

Pirtle, R. 87, **88**, **89**, 90, 95
pitch alteration 126
Plus One (DJ) 53, 54, 56, 57, 59, 61–2, 62
poetics 72–3
Pogo (DJ) 31, 46, 48
postmodernism/modernism 25–8
Presentation of Self in Everyday Life, The
    (Goffman) 55
Prime Cuts 53, 55–6, 57, 58–9, 64, 136–7
Prince, Tony 41
production and consumption, turntablism
    as both 27
progress and turntablism 26
provocative creativity 57
punchphasing 44, 114, 126, 135, 141–2

Q-Bert (DJ) 46–7, 94

Radar, notation developed by 82–4, 93–4,
    94–5
record tapping 126
records
    choice of 34
    early experiments with 17–18
    physical properties of 19–20
recycling, turntablism as 27–8
Reggae musicians 24, 25
rehearsals 106–12, 118–22, 130–31
reusing/recycling, turntablism as 27–8
rewinding 24
Reyes, Javier 11
rhythmic techniques 45–8
risk taking in groups 58
Roc Raida (DJ) 47–8
Rocc (DJ) 39
role allocation in groups 55–6, 63–4, 104,
    142–3
routines, analysis of
    characteristics of routines 140–45
    collective creation process 104–12,
        117–22, 129–31
    devising framework 138–9
    DMU Crew 103–18, *112*, *113*, **116**,
        145–6
    final rehearsals and performance
        111–12, 122, 131
    general properties of routine 112, *112*,
        122–3, *123*, 132, *132*

group organisation 112, 122, 131
manipulation techniques 114–15, *116*,
    125–8, *127*, 135–7, *136*, 141–2
Mixologists routine 117–28, *123*, *124*,
    125, *127*
phase 1 rehearsals 106–8, 120–21,
    130–31
phase 2 rehearsals 108–11, 121–2,
    130–31
pre-devising administration 104,
    117–18, 129
preliminary rehearsals 105–6, 118–20,
    129–30
relationships between parts 143–4
roles and responsibilities in groups
    142–3
sample choice for routine 113, *113*,
    123–4, *124*, 133, 133–4, 140–41
Scratch Perverts 129–38, *132*, *133*, *136*
sectional, routines as 140
structure of routine 113–14, 125, *125*,
    134–5
structure within sections 143
texture 116–17, 128, 137–8, 144–5
Ruminations (KRS-One) 9

sample choice for routine 113, *113*, 123–4,
    124, *133*, 133–4, 140–41
Schaeffer, Pierre 20–21, 25, 32, 33, 34, 35
scratch notation 82–4
Scratch Perverts
    binary form 143
    chain form 143
    characteristics of routines 140–45
    collective action 63
    collective action process 129–31
    common artistic ground 54
    competitions 63
    competitive ethic 57
    compositional process, analysis of
        129–38, *132*, *133*, *137*
    creative work 60
    devising framework 138–9
    DMU Crew compared to 145–6
    final rehearsals and performance 131
    formation of 53
    general properties of routine 132, *132*
    group organisation 131

layering technique 143
manipulation techniques 135–7, *136*,
    141–2, 142–3
negotiation of a new vision 58–9, 60
New York, Sept 1999 129–38, *132*,
    133, *137*
phase 1 and 2 rehearsals 130–31
preliminary rehearsals 129–30
questioning label of 'turntablism' 57–8
reasons for choosing 2
rebellion against authority 56–7
relationships between parts of routine
    144
role allocation in 55–6
sample choice for routine *133*, 133–4,
    140–41
structure of routine 134–5, 143
texture 137–8, 144–5
scratching 30, 45–7, 114–15, 126, 135,
    141, 142
Shiftee (DJ) 39
slip-cueing 22
sociological studies of hip-hop music 1–2,
    71–2
sticker loops 115, 142
Storm 12
storming 52
Stravinsky, Igor 17
structural techniques 43–5
structure
    of routines 113–14, 125, *125*, 134–5
    within sections 143
Sullivan, Arthur, Sir 16
Swift, Rob 48–9

Technics turntables 31
technology
    central role of 29
    digital, impact on DJ-ing 37–42
    experimentation, reasons for 35–7
    mixers 32
    as rapidly changing 30
    reconfiguration of existing 30
    records, choice of 34
    turntables 31, 32–4

use of 29–30
Teknyk 11
texture 116–17, 128, 137–8, 144–5
Theodore (DJ) 45–6
Toch, Ernst 18, 19, 20, 33, 35
transcription techniques
    for analysis of compositions 94–100,
        96, **97**, **98**, *99*, *100*
    functions of 92–4, **93**
    graphic notation 87–92, **88**, **89**
    limitations of for popular music 81–2
    need for standardised form 82
    staff notation 82–7, *85*, **86**, **87**
transformer scratch 46–7
TTM system 87, **88**, **89**, 90, 94, 95
turntable music
    early experiments 16–18
    emergence of 3–4
    history of experiments in 18–25
    methodology for research 2
    previous studies of 1–2
Turntable Transcription Methodology
    (TTM system) 87, **88**, **89**, 90, 94,
    95
turntables
    choice of 32–4
    evolution of 31
    experimentation, reasons for 35–7
turntablism
    as both production and consumption 27
    digital technology, impact of 40–42
    emergence of term 4
    and experimentation 26–7
    and innovation 26–7
    and progress 26
    questioning label of 57–8
    as reusing/recycling 27–8

Varèse, Edgar 19
Vegas, Tony 29–30, 46, 53, 54, 55–6, 56,
    57, 58–9, 60–61, 130, 131
Venum 11

Webber, Stephen, notation developed by
    86, **86**, **87**